A GREAT and TERRIBLE *Love*

A SPIRITUAL JOURNEY INTO THE ATTRIBUTES OF GOD

MARK GALLI

BakerBooks

a division of Baker Publishing Group
Grand Rapids, Michigan

© 2009 by Mark Galli

Published by Baker Books
a division of Baker Publishing Group
P.O. Box 6287, Grand Rapids, MI 49516-6287
www.bakerbooks.com

Paperback edition published 2010
ISBN 978-0-8010-7248-2

Printed in the United States of America

The Library of Congress has cataloged the hardcover editon as follows:
Galli, Mark
    A great and terrible love : a spiritual journey into the attributes of God / Mark Galli.
      p. cm.
    Includes bibliographical references.
    ISBN 978-0-8010-1295-2 (cloth)
    1. God (Christianity)—Attributes. I. Title.
BT130.G35 2009
231′.4—dc22   2008041333

10 11 12 13 14 15 16   7 6 5 4 3 2 1

To Ashley and Mary Woodiwiss,
who more than most have known
a great and terrible love.

Contents

Part 3: Attributes of Love

Foreword

We are homo sapiens, the creatures who know, or who want to know, or who think we know. We are the creatures who solve puzzles, who read Agatha Christie, who invent telescopes and microscopes and linear accelerators, who go to class and take tests and read textbooks and measure and question and test and muse and argue. We can't help ourselves. We want to know.

But what is worth knowing? Living in the Information Age has not demonstrably satisfied our curiosity nor made us wiser. Very smart people keep doing very foolish things with their lives.

A long time ago the most influential teacher who ever lived said one subject above all is worth pursuing: "Now this is eternal life; that they may know you, the only true God, and Jesus Christ, whom you have sent." He didn't mean (as I used to think growing up) that you get to go to heaven if you know certain things about God. He meant that knowing God—being able to think about and increasingly understand and experience and interact with and delight in this being of inconceivable goodness—is itself the greatest activity, the greatest relationship, the ultimate fulfillment of human existence. Aquinas said that theology is the queen of the sciences, not because he was a theologian (well, maybe a little), but because all other questions are included under its purview. There is no study that does not, eventually, lead to knowing something more about God.

We are the creatures who want to know. Of course, knowing God is something that requires more than just our heads. When I was a graduate student in clinical psychology I had a supervisor who advised me that when working with a sociopath you should never claim to be motivated by the desire to help. Tell them you're doing it for money. Because they are not capable of altruism, they are not capable of perceiving altruism, and will always attribute other motivations to people—even Mother Theresa. Our character limits our capacity to perceive, to know. Or, to put it another way, "No one can see God's face and live."

But if knowing God involves more than just our minds, it does not involve less. Thinking hard, deeply, systematically, passionately, and humbly about God is the best thinking we can do. God himself wants us to do this, not so that we can get the answers right on the Eternal Theology quiz, but because only when our minds have a clear sense of who God is are we able to think the kinds of thoughts that allow us to live with freedom and confidence and clarity.

And so the book you hold now is a part of the longest and most important conversation held by the human race: What is God like? Persons—even human ones—are both the easiest and the hardest objects of our knowing. Easy because (unlike quarks and cats) they can reveal themselves to us through words. Hard because they have a depth and mystery unlike any other piece of creation. And God is the summit of this paradox. Who can know God? He is infinite, transcendent, perfect, the occupant of the Other Side of the greatest chasm of all.

And yet . . . he is closer than we can imagine. Closer than the air we breathe. Not even separated by flesh and bones. Closer than any human being could ever be.

And he wants to be known.

So enough with the preliminaries. Read on.

We are the creatures who want to know.

John Ortberg

Acknowledgments

I wish to thank Marci Hintz and David Handy for reading an early draft of this manuscript and offering critiques that have made this a better book.

I thank my editor, Bob Hosack, who has once again shown patience with a writer who doesn't seem to know the meaning of the word *deadline*. While I wandered and doubted the book's vision at times, Bob also held my hands to the publishing fire to put my original ideas into words.

I thank Wendy Wetzel and Kristin Kornoelje, whose careful editing has made this book easier to read and has saved me from not a few embarrassing mistakes.

I remain indebted to my wife. She has every right to complain (but never does) about a husband who should pay more attention to her. Her patience and understanding of this lonely calling of writing have made yet another book possible. I have once again committed a kind of adultery, lavishing my affections on the making of books rather than the love of my life. For this grace, I remain deeply grateful.

Introduction

Who then are you, my God? ... Most high, utterly
good, utterly powerful, most omnipotent, most
merciful.

Augustine[1]

We are desperate for a great and terrible love.
We need a great love, one that captures our
imagination—and transcends it. The philosopher Anselm
offered this proof for God's existence: God is that which
nothing greater can be conceived. We need a love that is
greater than we can even conceive.

We are a desperately lonely people, in a lifelong search for
someone who will listen without judgment; who will embrace
without conditions; who will give us permission to be who
we are—sordid, sinful, lost, confused; who will not inter-
rupt when we admit our adultery or describe our schemes
of revenge or explain the wicked intricacies of our motives.
We don't want more advice. We don't want to be fixed. We
don't need a seven-step plan for a better life. We need a love
so great that it just listens with an empathy and offers an

embrace that says it's okay to be, in the words of the Book of Common Prayer, "a miserable sinner."

We also need a terrible love. A terrible love "causing great fear and alarm," like a terrible bolt of lightning. A terrible love that is "extremely formidable," like responsibilities that are terrible in their weight. A terrible love that is "intense" and "extreme," like a life that paid so terrible a price. And yes, a terrible love that is "unpleasant and disagreeable" at times, like having a terrible time at a party.[2]

We are a desperately inadequate people. We know all too well all too often what we are called by divine fiat to do. From the daily calls to clean up another's mess to the life calls of serving others in the home and in the world, we know what we are supposed to do, and a part of us wants to do it.

But sometimes sloth stalls obedience to the call—we just don't have the energy to love another minute. We need a love that will strike us like a bolt of lightning, to get our hearts racing with the will to move.

Sometimes the problem is selfishness—some days we just don't care. We need a love that can help us carry the great weight of the responsibility to love.

Sometimes it is hopelessness—we have failed so many times in so many ways that we just cannot imagine that making another effort will do any good. We need a love that is so intense and extreme, it makes despair an impossibility.

A love like this will be unpleasant and disagreeable at times, but the kingdom party is not decorated in Mary Englebreit motifs. We need a love that will offer an embrace that braces us to do the unpleasant and disagreeable things we are called to do.

In the famous book and movie *The Wizard of Oz*, the Scarecrow, the Tin Man, and the Lion approached in fear and trembling the Wizard of Oz, who with signs and wonders and a thundering voice described himself as "the great and terrible Oz." It was his terribleness that drew the three companions to him and sent them forth on a mission in the course of which they slew the Wicked Witch. It was his greatness that, in the end, embraced them with mercy and kindness.

I was preaching on that most enigmatic of passages—where God tells Abraham to sacrifice his son Isaac and then prevents him from doing the very thing he commanded (see Gen. 22:1–14). I spoke candidly about the mystery of God's sovereign will, about how difficult it is to discern what God is doing and why he's doing it. I chastised our weak attempts to explain and defend God's inexplicable behavior, both in Scripture and in light of then recent world tragedies. I reminded the congregation that the Bible is less interested in justifying God's behavior than in simply acknowledging his sovereignty:

> I am the LORD, and there is no other.
> I form light and create darkness,
> I make weal and create woe;
> I the LORD do all these things.
>
> Isaiah 45:6–7

The congregation was riveted, not because of my delivery but, as I later found out, by the plain description of the terribleness of God. Afterward some extolled my courage for broaching a topic that puzzled them, others thanked me for helping them break through a personal crisis, and others still said they were simply moved for inexplicable reasons.

It suggested to me once again the recurring relevance of one theme of my first book in this series, *Jesus Mean and Wild: The Unexpected Love of an Untamable God*: we are not attracted to God merely because of his great love. We instinctively know we need more than a divine grandfather who pats us on the head, or a cosmic bellhop who fulfills all our wishes, or a buddy and traveling companion. There is also something strangely and fearsomely attractive about the one who forms light and creates darkness, whose love is not only great but terrible.

Almost a half century ago, A. W. Tozer lamented that "The church has surrendered her once lofty concept of God and has substituted for it one so low, so ignoble, as to be utterly unworthy of thinking, worshipping men. This she has done not deliberately, but little by little and without her knowledge; and her very unawareness makes her situation all the more tragic."[3]

Tozer was shaking his finger at the church, but today we don't need a shaking finger, for we nod in assent when we hear this. We know from experience we are poorer as individuals and churches. The simplistic view of God, as Tozer suggested, "is the cause of a hundred lesser evils everywhere among us," including the loss of "our spirit of worship and our ability to withdraw inwardly to meet God in adoring silence."[4]

He penned these lines in his classic *The Knowledge of the Holy* almost a half century ago. Another classic of the era, J. B. Phillips's *Your God Is Too Small*, argued along similar lines, but he was thinking more evangelistically: "Many men and women today are living, often with inner dissatisfaction, without any faith in God at all. This is not because they are particularly wicked or selfish . . . but because they have not found with their adult minds a God big enough . . . to command their highest admiration and respect, and consequently their willing co-operation."[5]

Both these authors were saying in their own way that we need not a warm and fuzzy God but one who offers a great and terrible love. They argued their point by writing about the attributes of God. Fifty years later, I believe a similar book is needed.

The attributes of God—omniscience, omnipresence, and so forth—have fallen on hard times. The philosophically inclined have deconstructed them one by one. They've asked penetrating questions like "How can an immutable God, one who doesn't change, answer prayer?" And "How can we have free will if an omniscient God already knows what we're going to do?" And "How can an omnipotent and all-loving God allow evil?" They've noted how much these divine attributes owe to Greek thought and how words like *immutable* and *omniscient* don't even appear in the Bible. They've suggested that Christian theology took a wrong turn at the beginning, abandoning the more personal God of the Bible for a god of philosophers.

There is some truth to these charges. If the classic attributes are not handled with discernment, God will indeed appear as a philosophical idea—distant and unapproachable. This indeed has happened from time to time in Christian circles, so anxious were preachers and teachers to guard the majesty of God.

But the theologians who have most eloquently expounded on the classic attributes—Augustine, Aquinas, and Anselm, for example—never abandoned the personal God of the Bible. They managed to integrate their philosophical training with their theological understanding to give us a full-orbed and compelling picture of the biblical God.

In this book I accept implicitly most of their discussions. I've read the philosophical arguments for a complete revision of the classic attributes, but I find them generally unpersuasive and unbiblical. Naturally, theological knowledge continues to grow, so that our understanding of some of the attributes has become more nuanced. But I've not been convinced that we can do better than many of the classical expressions, which combine intellectual rigor with fierce devotion. Take one passage from Augustine:

> Who then are you, my God? . . . Most high, utterly good, utterly powerful, most omnipotent, most merciful and most just, deeply hidden yet most intimately present, perfection of both beauty and strength, stable and incomprehensible, immutable and yet changing all things, never new, never old, making everything new.[6]

The fierce devotion to the God of these attributes is what most interests me. I want to discuss the attributes not philosophically as much as theologically and spiritually, to attempt a spiritual theology. I assume that these classic attributes are both intellectual stumbling blocks and spiritually enticing. They paradoxically repel and attract. For example, I describe in one chapter how an omnipresent God both intimidates and comforts us and in another how the inscrutability of God both frightens us and draws us closer to him. I assume the theological reality of the attribute on my way to unveiling God's great and terrible love.

The book is divided into three parts: the theological attributes, the biblical attributes, and the attributes of love.

The theological attributes include those that come freighted with abstract and intimidating words: immutability, omniscience, and so forth. While these words do not appear in the Bible, they remain sensible shorthand descriptions of the God who is portrayed in the Bible.

The biblical attributes are no less theological, but they do concern words that can be found in the biblical text: mercy, righteousness, judgment, and wrath.

I will try to show <u>that all the attributes are, in the end, attributes of love</u>, but the three discussed under the final section—Trinity, suffering, and mystery—strike me as the ones that reveal the love of God in ways that are particularly striking today.

If you read five books on the attributes, you will find them organized in five different ways. What readers will soon discover is how the different attributes slide into one another, that to talk about omnipresence is also to talk about omniscience, and so forth. So at one level all the attributes are like the mystery of the Trinity, where multiple and discrete ideas are both many and one.

Nor is this list exhaustive. I've chosen the attributes that strike me as interesting to think about right now—thus, for example, I begin with today's most thorny attribute, the immutability of God. In another five years, I might come up with a different list, ordered in another way. Such is the nature of spiritual theology, which uses the insights of the systematic theologian to talk about the ever-changing spiritual realities of men and women who long to know the fullness of God.

As I reread the book before sending it off to my publisher, I was surprised at the variety of approaches I used. This is partly the result of writing a book over a two-year period. But as I tried to make the approaches more consistent, I found the very nature of the chapters changing. It occurred to me that there was some method to this madness, that different attributes call for different approaches because of the spiritual place we find ourselves in today. So, for example, the chapter on the righteous God has to traffic in some rather heavy biblical theology to get us to think about the word *righteous* less like twentieth-century North Americans and more like New Testament people. But other chapters are but ruminations about the theme, weaving biblical allusions with personal experience.

Despite the outline, this book is not a progression but a series of essays. Readers can dip in and out at will and not lose a great deal. I hope this will make it more useful for study groups that would like to spend but four to six or eight weeks with the book.

However the book is used, personally or in study groups, my aim is pastoral. I wish that readers would grasp not only the Augustinian vision of God—"Most high, utterly good, utterly powerful, most omnipotent, most merciful"[7]—but also Augustine's lasting insight that this God has made us for himself and that our hearts are restless until we find our rest in his great and terrible love.

Mark Galli
Sixth week in Easter, AD 2008

PART 1

Theological Attributes

1

Responsive Control (Immutable)

For I the LORD do not change; therefore you, O children of Jacob, are not consumed.

Malachi 3:6

God is one on whom we can depend.

That's the premise of any book about God (unless it's a book denying God, of course). I want to establish, among other things, what it is about God that we can know and trust and count on—though I will often traffic in paradox and mystery to unravel what it means that God is dependable. He does not change. He is immutable.

That would be reason enough to start with this attribute. But there is another. The traditional attribute that we call divine immutability has fallen on harder times than most attributes, with entire theologies (process and openness theology) trying to make change the crucial characteristic of God. Such theologies are not mere academic exercises. They are trying to address serious human problems.

There is the philosophical puzzle, of course. God is said to be unchanging. And yet the Bible says he created the heavens and the earth (see Gen. 1:1). That act, of course, implies changes of all sorts: from deciding to create to creating, from existing in eternity to having a relationship to changing time and space, and so forth. How can a God who is changeless inaugurate a universe characterized by change?

It's an interesting problem, but it's not nearly as interesting as the pastoral problem that confronts anyone who bows in prayer to this God: if God is unchanging, why bother to make requests of him? If the all-powerful and all-wise God is set on a certain course, it is hard to imagine why the prayers of stupid and selfish creatures deserve a hearing, let alone a response.

The answer would be simple—i.e., don't petition God; it's pointless—if it weren't for the repeated affirmations of the one who is said to have an intimate knowledge of this God. When teaching about prayer, Jesus once told a story:

> In a certain city there was a judge who neither feared God nor respected man. And there was a widow in that city who kept coming to him and saying, "Give me justice against my adversary." For a while he refused, but afterward he said to himself, "Though I neither fear God nor respect man, yet because this widow keeps bothering me, I will give her justice, so that she will not beat me down by her continual coming."
>
> Luke 18:2–5

Jesus concluded, "Hear what the unrighteous judge says. *And will not God give justice to his elect, who cry to him day and night?* Will he delay long over them? I tell you, he will give justice to them speedily" (Luke 18:6–8, emphasis added).

Another time, he used both analogy and argument to drive home the point:

Ask, and it will be given to you; seek, and you will find; knock, and it will be opened to you. For everyone who asks receives, and the one who seeks finds, and to the one who knocks it will be opened. Or which one of you, if his son asks him for bread, will give him a stone? Or if he asks for a fish, will give him a serpent? If you then, who are evil, know how to give good gifts to your children, how much more will your Father who is in heaven give good things to those who ask him!

Matthew 7:7–11

Jesus paints a picture of a Father God who longs to fulfill the requests of his needy children. He appears to be not immutable at all but poised to do things he had no intention of doing until requested.

That is not all. This picture implies that God is subject to the whims of his children, those described by Jesus here as "evil" and elsewhere as "faithless and twisted" (Matt. 17:17). God is not only subject to change, suggests Jesus, but is prompted to change by creatures of questionable character.

This can't bode well for the universe.

Jesus stands in a long line of Hebrew prophets who had been making more or less the same point for centuries. Take that most entertaining of stories from that literature, the story of Jonah.

Jonah is told by God to go to Nineveh and "call out against it, for their evil has come up before me" (Jonah 1:2). The implication is clear: Nineveh has been so wicked that it will suffer God's wrath. Jonah finds this commission so distasteful that he boards a ship headed in the opposite direction.

God responds by stirring up a violent, life-threatening storm. The crew, discerning that Jonah is the cause of their troubles, tosses him overboard.

God responds by sending a great fish to swallow Jonah. From the belly of this great fish, Jonah repents of his disobedience.

23

God responds by sticking his finger down the throat of the whale, and the whale hurls Jonah onto dry land.

Jonah begins preaching judgment to Nineveh, and the people of Nineveh repent.

God responds once more: he puts his judgment on hold.

In short, God constantly reacts throughout the story, and in the end he changes his mind. This does not look like a picture of immutable divinity.

In fact, all through the Scriptures, one almost gets the sense that this God not only changes, he seems addicted to it and even codependent on us. God comes off as a bleeding heart liberal, a mad philanthropist, a god who will do an about-face at the least prodding of his narcissistic, selfish, and often evil children. What type of heavenly parent is that? An overly indulgent one who can't seem to say no to his children, who will change his intentions at the drop of a humble prayer.

Yet if we peel back this layer, we find beneath another painting of an altogether different God. This is the almighty God who, through Jesus, intends to bring history to a cataclysmic conclusion, and there is no hint that he will be swayed from his course. After describing the events that will lead up to the judgment, Jesus says this:

> Then will appear in heaven the sign of the Son of Man, and then all the tribes of the earth will mourn, and they will see the Son of Man coming on the clouds of heaven with power and great glory. And he will send out his angels with a loud trumpet call, and they will gather his elect from the four winds, from one end of heaven to the other.
>
> Matthew 24:30–31

And to ensure that his listeners grasp the inevitability of this scenario, Jesus concludes, "Heaven and earth will pass away, but my words will not pass away" (Matt. 24:35).

Parable after parable that follows assumes that people need to be ready, for the judgment is indeed coming and history will culminate in the coming of the kingdom of heaven. The arrival of this kingdom is not subject to the whims of fickle people. When Jesus teaches his disciples to pray, he includes a phrase to remind us of the unswaying nature of God's purpose: "Thy kingdom come, Thy will be done in earth, as it is in heaven" (Matt. 6:10 KJV).

This assured reality is often portrayed today as cause for comfort, but for the biblical writers, it was an occasion for sober reflection. Note, for example, the context of the one biblical verse that is said more than any other to support the immutability of God:

> Then I will draw near to you for judgment. I will be a swift witness against the sorcerers, against the adulterers, against those who swear falsely, against those who oppress the hired worker in his wages, the widow and the fatherless, against those who thrust aside the sojourner, and do not fear me, says the LORD of hosts.
>
> For I the LORD do not change; therefore you, O children of Jacob, are not consumed. From the days of your fathers you have turned aside from my statutes and have not kept them. Return to me, and I will return to you, says the LORD of hosts.
>
> Malachi 3:5–7

Or take this passage from the New Testament:

> Remember your leaders, those who spoke to you the word of God. Consider the outcome of their way of life, and imitate their faith. Jesus Christ is the same yesterday and today and forever. Do not be led away by diverse and strange teachings.
>
> Hebrews 13:7–9

In this light, God is not an overindulgent parent continually spoiling his bratty children but a stern and just judge who is Lord of his creation. "He is unchanged, blessed be his name, in his justice," preached C. H. Spurgeon. "Just and holy was he in the past; just and holy is he now."[1] He does not respond to history, which like a river is constantly running over its banks. Instead, God steadily channels that river toward the kingdom of heaven. We can fight the current—and drown trying. Or we can order our lives to move with the current of God.

When we see this layer of the painting, we are back to the problem of prayer: why make petitions to an unchangeable God? As one theologian put it:

> God dwells in perfect bliss outside the sphere of time and space. . . . [He] remains essentially unaffected by creaturely events and experiences. He is untouched by the disappointment, sorrow or suffering of his creatures. Just as his sovereign will brooks no opposition, his serene tranquility knows no interruption.[2]

The answer seems to lie in the paradox of prayer: God responds to his people in order to fulfill his unchanging purpose.

The story of Jonah, then, is not merely an entertaining parable but a metaphor of universal significance. It is our story, and we sometimes play the role of Jonah and sometimes that of the Ninevites. God intends good for the people of Nineveh. And God will work with what he's got—even the fickle, proud, and resentful—to make that happen. He will move heaven and earth, sky and sea, and even the great creatures that inhabit them—anything and everything to guarantee that his unchanging purpose is achieved.

His purpose is nothing less than the salvation of humankind—salvation from everything from our self-destructive narcissism to the mass destructions brought on by injustice and oppression. Salvation for new life in a rehabilitated earth.

Prayer and the unchanging purpose of God embrace in two ways.

First and foremost, in prayer we align ourselves with the unchanging will of God; we learn to swim with the current and not against it; we learn to say, "Not my will, but thine be done."

Aligning our wills with God's is not a matter of meek abdication, of mindless submission to the power and wisdom of an almighty divinity. It begins by boldly accepting the invitation to make our desires known to God: "Ask, and it will be given to you" (Matt. 7:7). It is not until after Jesus pleads that the cup of suffering be removed that he finally discerns that it is not God's will that it be removed. Only after wrestling with God does he relent of his desires.

God's unchanging purposes, then, are discovered in the argument of prayer. To reduce prayer to begging God to fulfill our desires is childish. To abdicate to God without first acknowledging our desires is to deny our humanity, the person created and shaped by God. Pure acquiescence is often portrayed as the most saintly posture of prayer, but in reality God invites us to argue with him. And it is through the argument that knowledge of God's will emerges.

This is the dynamic of all relationships. It is only in the back-and-forth of honest, passionate conversation that deeper understanding emerges. Only by expressing our desires and views and hearing a challenge do we begin to see that our desires and views have richer features than we had first imagined. Only in argument do we see where our desire has become selfishness and where our opinion is but ignorance.

Even more so when we argue with God. Through the argument of prayer we better understand ourselves as well as the unchanging nature and purpose of God.

Prayer is also the means by which we fulfill one of God's unchanging purposes—that we might participate with our

27

Creator in his work of creation: "Let us make man in our image, after our likeness; and let them have dominion" (Gen. 1:26). Our very nature mirrors that of our Creator: we have dominion. We are to participate with God in managing the creation and in welcoming the new creation, doing so in thought, word, and deed.

This too is a paradoxical calling. For we are the ones responsible for the river of history spilling over the banks that God intends for it to stay in. At the same time, God gives us the authority and power to shore up the levees broken by our own foolishness. In this work, we need a word that calls to our attention our foolishness and its consequences, the courage to acknowledge our foolishness and its consequences, and the moral strength to begin the work anew—such things that only come from God in prayer.

And in managing creation and welcoming the new creation, we are given great latitude, and in this, prayer plays a crucial role.

We can liken it to a father and his son. The father wants his son to participate in athletics, but he does not really care which sport his son undertakes. The father may suggest baseball, and a dutiful son (thinking his only option was submissive obedience) would acquiesce and sign up for Little League. But if the son were to say he'd rather play tennis or basketball or golf, the father would be more than happy to oblige.

Whenever we pray, we petition a fatherly God who gives his people great latitude. Like a loving father, he will not grant us every desire, for some are clearly outside his will. Neither will he ignore our wishes, as if our wills did not matter. He created our wills with the intent that we should use them, so he wants us to employ them. But within the parameters of his unchanging purpose for us and for all of humankind, he grants many a request.

This astounding reality—that prayer participates in the unchanging purposes of God—does not answer the philosophical questions about why God fails to answer many prayers that would, it seems, be in his kingdom interest. Why did he not heal the wicked cancer of a friend, or why does he seem silent about sexual trafficking and other great social evils?

But the doctrine of God's immutability then draws us into a presence that reassures. As Søren Kierkegaard prayed, "Thou who art unchangeable in love."[3] Or as A. W. Tozer put it,

> In coming to him at any time, we need not wonder whether we shall find him in a receptive mood. He is always receptive to misery and need, as well as to love and faith. . . . Neither does he change his mind about anything. Today, this moment, he feels toward his creatures, toward babies, toward the sick, the fallen, the sinful, exactly as he did when he sent his only begotten Son into the world to die for mankind.[4]

Like all the attributes, God's immutability holds a paradox and a power we will not begin to grasp until we trust ourselves to an unchanging God, who remains immutably and paradoxically in control *and* responsive—both "Jesus Christ is the same yesterday and today and forever" (Heb. 13:8) and the one who invites us with, "Ask, and it will be given to you" (Matt. 7:7).

2

Right- and Left-Handed Power (Omnipotent)

> Behold, I am the LORD, the God of all flesh. Is anything too hard for me?
>
> Jeremiah 32:27

I f God were not omnipotent, we'd have to invent omnipotence and pin the attribute on him. We need a God of limitless power.

We long for unparalleled divine power because we are only too aware of our unmitigated weakness. We cannot govern our lives, let alone our world. Even when we achieve good, we cannot do so without the bad leaking out all over the place. Think welfare—it alleviated grinding poverty but created a culture of dependency. Think warfare—even the most just wars shed innocent blood. In the one area over which we imagine we retain some sovereignty, our personal lives, control remains elusive: even the most holy, as they are quick to confess, are plagued by ugly habits and compulsive narcissism.

Our weakness is so very weak, and we long for a power to heal us inside and out, for goodness to reach into the depths of our souls, for justice to rule to the ends of the earth. And we locate that power in God.

Power: "The ability or capacity to perform or act effectively. . . . The ability or official capacity to exercise control; authority." The word comes from the Old French *pooir*, "to be able, power," and from the Vulgar Latin *potēre*, "to be able."[1] Yes, that's what we want—an able God.

Not coincidently, the Bible reveals a God who is able.

From the opening words of Genesis—"In the beginning God created the heaven and the earth" (Gen. 1:1 KJV)—to the closing of the book of Revelation—"the Lord God omnipotent reigneth" (Rev. 19:6 KJV)—the Bible showcases a divine being who possesses unparalleled power.

This is the God who, without any materials to work with, fashions a universe. He destroys the pretentions of the haughty in Babel and creates life in the barren womb of Sarah. The biblical God causes famines, instigates plagues, divides waters, and destroys armies. He demands obedience of his people, and when ignored, he raises up other nations, who drag his people into exile—and then, when it is in his good will, God ushers them back to their land.

This God does not strain nor sweat but performs such majestic deeds as easily as people talk. As the psalmist put it, God "spoke and it came to be; he commanded, and it stood firm" (Ps. 33:9). It is no wonder we find Jeremiah sensing God telling him, "Behold, I am the LORD, the God of all flesh. Is anything too hard for me?" (Jer. 32:27).

Apparently not, for this God shows up in the New Testament as one who makes possible both miraculous conception and unexpected resurrection. The birth of the God-man is accompanied by an army of angels, and the life of the God-man is characterized by healing the blind, curing the lame, casting out demons, and raising the dead.

A Roman centurion, a man who understands power, grasps intuitively the nature of Jesus's authority. When Jesus offers to walk to the man's home and heal his son, the centurion refuses:

> Lord, do not trouble yourself, for I am not worthy to have you come under my roof. Therefore I did not presume to come to you. But say the word, and let my servant be healed. For I too am a man set under authority, with soldiers under me: and I say to one, "Go," and he goes; and to another, "Come," and he comes; and to my servant, "Do this," and he does it.
>
> Luke 7:6–8

Jesus marveled at this, and told those standing nearby that "not even in Israel have I found such faith" (Luke 7:9)—faith in Jesus's power.

We smile knowingly when we read that Jesus's contemporaries looked for a political messiah who would usher in the kingdom with the sword. Yet for the longest time in Jesus's ministry, it was an easy mistake to make. Jesus comes across as one who very much looks like the God of Israel, who the prophet Isaiah said "comes with might, and his arm rules for him; behold, his reward is with him, and his recompense before him" (Isa. 40:10).

So it makes sense that when the early church wanted to sum up the faith, it would revert to words that expressed God's power and authority: "We believe in God the Father almighty. . . . in Jesus Christ our Lord. . . . in the Holy Spirit, the Lord and giver of life."

In the Bible, God's almighty power is the cause of much awe and praise; it is also the cause of much lament. Many of these expressions of lament cannot be understood apart from a bedrock belief in God's omnipotence. When injustice prevails in the prophet Habakkuk's day, he understandably whines,

> O LORD, how long shall I cry for help,
>   and you will not hear?
> Or cry to you "Violence!"
>   and you will not save?
> Why do you make me see iniquity,
>   and why do you idly look at wrong?
> Destruction and violence are before me;
>   strife and contention arise.
> So the law is paralyzed,
>   and justice never goes forth.
> For the wicked surround the righteous;
>   so justice goes forth perverted.
>
> Habakkuk 1:2–4

In short, where is almighty God when unlimited power is most needed?

In our own day we find this question dressed up in fresh garb: How can a good and all-powerful God allow so much evil? We today do not presuppose God's omnipotence, but we continue to long for it. What we're wondering is, *Is God not so powerful after all? Are we left alone to manage this mess?*

We're wondering, in other words, if God is really left-handed.

When the biblical writers reach for a metaphor of divine power, they talk about God's "right hand." The psalmist proclaims that the Lord will save his anointed "with the saving might of his right hand" (Ps. 20:6), and the author of Exodus says, "Your right hand, O LORD, glorious in power, your right hand, O LORD, shatters the enemy" (Exod. 15:6).

While the New Testament gives us snapshots of God's right hand, we see another picture begin to emerge—evidence of God's left hand.

Omnipotence in the form of a helpless baby.

The refusal of Jesus to use raw miracle to satisfy his hunger or to prove himself, and his decided lack of interest in the devil's offer of "all the kingdoms of the world and their glory" (Matt. 4:8).

His repeated refusal to retaliate in the face of injustice, from his arrest to the crucifixion.

The first glimmer of the truth that it is in dying that we live.

This looks not like God's omnipotent right hand but like the impotence of a left-handed God. The type of God that makes one wonder if he's really got things under control.

Or a God who wants to startle us out of our ideas of omnipotence.

Father Leslie Chadd, in an article titled "God's Left Hand," summed up the nature of left-handed power:

At the centre of it is a baby in a makeshift cot in a mucky stable, before whom the kings, symbols of the world's right-handed wisdom and power, bend the knee. He is the Messiah who turns all our cherished right-handed ideas upside down and says that children are at the top of the pile, not at the bottom of it. He is the one who rebukes the strong right-handed Boanerges brothers who would knock out those difficult Samaritans with a divine thunderbolt. He is the King who could call an army of angels to his aid but who refuses the help of Peter's sword-bearing right arm. He is the God who will not slay his enemies with his strong right arm but who says instead "if there is any killing to be done, it will be done to me, not by me."[2]

This leads some to assume that true disciples of Jesus must reject power, because after all, when the God-man was offered it, he refused. Any dabbling in power or associating

God with right-handed power is bowing to the god of this world and not the God who transcends it and its entire value structure in the cross.

Well, yes and no. The Gospels describe plenty of moments when Jesus did, in fact, use raw power, from healing lepers to calming storms to raising Lazarus from the dead. And as Paul said, Jesus "was declared to be the Son of God in power according to the Spirit of holiness by his resurrection from the dead" (Rom. 1:4).

What God is doing in the New Testament is not denying his right-handed power but helping us see and experience his left-handed power. Many suppose they can grasp the nature of divine power by magnifying the most powerful energy they know to the nth degree. That is to severely limit the nature of God's power.

What we see in light of the cross is that divine power is also revealed in suffering and death. The moments of apparent divine defeat are in fact moments of victory. When God looks most weak, that's when he's most omnipotent.

The question of Habakkuk—which is our question as well—is turned on its head. "How can an all-powerful God stand by and do nothing while the planet writhes in travail?" But of course, he isn't doing nothing. The very suffering of the planet has become his suffering, and divine suffering is always redemptive suffering. The apparent weakness of God during a tsunami or AIDS epidemic is like unto the God whose arms are nailed to the cross while onlookers mock his impotence.

So in the end, we've gotten the God we want—one who truly is all-powerful, one who is able. Our instincts were right after all. We didn't make this thing up. But we didn't exactly get omnipotence in the way we imagined it.

We still wish we lived in a time of glory and power, of miracle and might, as did Abraham and Moses, and Miriam and Mary, and the disciples in the upper room. But in these latter days, God has decided to reveal his power in weakness. This is the age we live in.

This certainly makes our lives interesting. On the one hand, it saves us from having to dig through history to try to prove that God is in charge of this mess. God has providentially ordered things so that history shows little evidence of his power. While we can never fathom why God is now making known his power in this hidden way, one or two things seem apparent.

One is that God wants us to move beyond faith in the all-powerful-God-who-rescues-us-magically-from-all-our-problems. This is the health-and-wealth god, the ten-steps-to-a-full-life god. This is the god who has nothing better to do than to make us happy. The religion that emerges when we worship this god is, in the end, a religion whose totem is the self. It is a religion about my life, my problems, my happiness. But God knows we need something bigger than this, so he's pulled away the crutch so that we might learn to love him and not his power.

The second thing is that God is trying to expand our understanding of the power we have. Since we are created in his image, we share something of his power. Sometimes we are called to wield the right arm.

We see the proper use of the right arm when a mother, by the force of her will, insists that her daughter not cross the street without holding hands. Or when a coach chews out a player for inattention. Or when a police officer chases down a thief. Or when soldiers attack a terrorist hideout.

And many times we are called to wield the left arm. When a coworker insults us and we do not retaliate. When a friend betrays us and we forgive. When a church is burned to the ground by a group that despises the faith.

Both arms are forms of power; both are able to get things done. Right-handed power can insist on obedience and justice, but it can't change people. Left-handed power cannot bring justice, but it can move hearts. Right-handed power brings order. Left-handed power transforms lives.

In this small way, we reflect the omnipotence of God, a God who aims to bring justice to the earth and to change human hearts, one by one. This God is not limited to right-handed power but is so powerful that even his apparent weakness is a sign that he is able to do that which he intends to accomplish.

3

Power
Incognito
(Immanent)

Here is the sea, great and wide,
  which teems with creatures innumerable,
  living things both small and great. . . .
These all look to you.

Psalm 104:25, 27

While God's power is revealed in weakness, the church continues to affirm the classic view: God's power also rules the universe. We not only respect this power, we honor and laud it, in ancient psalms:

For the LORD is a great God,
  and a great King above all gods.

Psalm 95:3

And in classic hymns:

> Praise to the Lord, the Almighty, the King of
> creation!
> O my soul, praise Him, for He is thy health and
> salvation![1]

Such praise points to a God who does something *to* this world and *to* us. The Bible also suggests that this power is plain for all to see:

> The heavens declare the glory of God,
>   and the sky above proclaims his handiwork.
> Day to day pours out speech,
>   and night to night reveals knowledge.
>
> Psalm 19:1–2

The apostle Paul says more or less the same thing in his letter to the church in Rome: "For his invisible attributes, namely, his eternal power and divine nature, have been clearly perceived, ever since the creation of the world, in the things that have been made" (Rom. 1:20).

Yet a lot of people fail to see God's power. Sometimes, like the parables that hide as much as they reveal, creation masks as much as it shows forth God's "invisible attributes." History can seem like a series of self-propelled events, and nature, a system of immutable laws that run on their own energy.

But if God's power can be known in weakness, it can also be known when it remains hidden. We may not consciously recognize the energy that makes our home habitable. The refrigerator hums quietly, the dishwasher cleans the utensils, the television entertains, and the lights enable us to read. It all seems so natural. But there is a power that makes all these commonplaces work, day in and day out. And there is an omnipotence that energizes all creation, upholding it moment by moment, even when we're not aware:

40

O LORD, how manifold are your works!
    In wisdom have you made them all;
    the earth is full of your creatures.
Here is the sea, great and wide,
    which teems with creatures innumerable,
    living things both small and great. . . .
These all look to you,
    to give them their food in due season.
When you give it to them, they gather it up;
    when you open your hand, they are filled with
        good things.
When you hide your face, they are dismayed;
    when you take away their breath, they die
        and return to their dust.
When you send forth your Spirit, they are created,
    and you renew the face of the ground.

Psalm 104:24–30

In this book, I play with both the transcendence and the immanence of God, his distance and his nearness. We cannot understand the one without the other. Like most great truths, we cannot fathom the fullness of these attributes without resorting to paradox. God is completely one—and yet triune. Jesus is fully human—and yet completely divine. God can be known truly as Father—and yet this Divine Being is beyond personality and is finally a mystery.

Here I want to suggest that God's power is completely *transcendent* (a power that comes from outside us and acts on us) and yet *immanent* (a power that is nearer to us than we are to ourselves). This paradox has a long and venerable history, and I have found the teaching of the Eastern Orthodox tradition the most helpful in thinking about it.

When the Eastern church fathers speak of God's transcendence, they talk about his *essence*, and they argue that in his essence, God is completely unknowable. The early church father John of Damascus said:

41

God, then, is infinite and incomprehensible, and all that is comprehensible about him is his infinity and incomprehensibility. . . . God does not belong to the class of existing things: not that he has no existence, but that he is above all existing things, nay above existence itself.[2]

Thus the Orthodox attraction to what is called "apophatic" spirituality, in which ignorance becomes the path to knowledge. Take this passage from Vladimir Lossky's *The Mystical Theology of the Eastern Church*:

If in seeing God one can know what one sees, then one has not seen God in himself but something intelligible, something which is inferior to him. It is by *unknowing* that one may know him who is above every object of knowledge.[3]

On the other hand, these same church fathers affirm that God can be known, and they ground this affirmation in Scripture: "No one has ever seen God; the only God, who is at the Father's side, he has made him known" (John 1:18). While we cannot know God in his *essence*, we can know him in his *energies*—that is, the various ways he makes himself known to us.

It is in the light of Jesus Christ, then, that we "clearly perceive" God's "eternal power and divine nature" (Rom. 1:20). As Paul put it, "there is one God, the Father, from whom are all things and for whom we exist, and one Lord, Jesus Christ, through whom are all things and through whom we exist" (1 Cor. 8:6). While God in his essence transcends all that exists, in his energies we can perceive that God is in all things, for everything that is springs from him and subsists in him.

Christian mystics have been those who, while acknowledging God as "unapproachable Light," try to discern the immanent presence of God within themselves. They are also the ones who wax most eloquent about the nearness of God in the very stuff of everyday life.

42

In the prayer attributed to Saint Patrick called "The Breast-plate of Saint Patrick" or *Lorica*, we read of a Christ who is found everywhere:

> Christ with me, Christ before me, Christ behind me,
>   Christ in me!
> Christ below me, Christ above me.
> Christ at my right, Christ at my left!
> Christ in breadth, Christ in length, Christ in height!
>
> Christ in the heart of everyone who thinks of me,
> Christ in the mouth of everyone who speaks to me,
> Christ in every eye that sees me,
> Christ in every ear that hears me![4]

Saint Francis's famous poem "The Canticle of Brother Sun" underscores his nature mysticism, his perception of God in all of creation:

> Be praised, my Lord, through all your creatures,
> especially through my lord Brother Sun,
> who brings the day; and you give light through him.
> And he is beautiful and radiant in all his splendor!
> Of you, Most High, he bears the likeness.
>
> Praised be You, my Lord, through Sister Moon
> and the stars, in heaven you formed them
> clear and precious and beautiful.
>
> Praised be You, my Lord, through Brother Wind,
> and through the air, cloudy and serene,
> and every kind of weather through which
> You give sustenance to Your creatures.
>
> Praised be You, my Lord, through Sister Water,
> which is very useful and humble and precious and
>   chaste.

> Praised be You, my Lord, through Brother Fire,
> through whom you light the night and he is beautiful
> and playful and robust and strong.

> Praised be You, my Lord, through Sister Mother
>   Earth,
> who sustains us and governs us and who produces
> varied fruits with colored flowers and herbs.[5]

The biblical story of creation is not important because it pinpoints the earth's geological age or because it teaches Intelligent Design. When the author of Genesis says, "In the beginning, God created the heavens and the earth" (1:1), it's the *beginning* not just as in the first moment of time but also in the sense that God is the ongoing cause of creation and the sustainer of creation.

Julian of Norwich, when meditating one day, was startled with this insight:

> He showed me . . . a little thing, the size of a hazelnut, on the palm of my hand, round like a ball. I looked at it thoughtfully and wondered, "What is this?" And the answer came, "It is all that is made." I marveled that it continued to exist and did not suddenly disintegrate; it was so small. And my mind supplied the answer, "It exists, both now, and for ever, because God loves it." In short, everything owes its existence to the love of God.
>
>   In this "little thing," I saw three truths. The first is that God made it; the second is that God loves it; and the third is that God sustains it.[6]

God is at the heart of each little thing in the universe, sustaining its existence moment by moment. Scientifically, we see cause and effect. But if we're attentive, we can also discern divine activity in, with, and under cause and effect, an energy that upholds all that is.

But let me be clear: though God is present in all things, the world is not God. That is pantheism. Instead the church, certainly its Eastern Orthodox wing, has taught an orthodox version of *panentheism*: God is *in* all things yet also *beyond and above* all things. As Saint Gregory Palamas put it, "He is everywhere and nowhere, he is everything and nothing." A Cistercian monk of New Clairvaux said something similar: "God is at the core. God is other than the core. God is within the core, and all through the core, and beyond the core, closer to the core than the core."[7]

I am using hyperbole here, of course, when I say "in, with, and under." This is the language Martin Luther used to describe how Christ is present in the eucharistic bread and wine. This is the deepest way in which Christ comes to us. In the bread and wine, we receive God in his fullness, the God of creation and incarnation, the God of the cross and the resurrection, the God of history and the God of the coming kingdom.

Without the revelation of Jesus Christ, nature would be experienced as a power arbitrary and cruel. Only in light of Christ's brutal death on the cross can we contemplate earthquakes and thunder, hurricanes and tornadoes as signs of a fierce but loving God. Only in light of the Eucharist, where Christ is truly present in, with, and under the bread and wine, can we discern God's presence in the terror and splendor of nature.

To discern God's power in nature, we start by paying attention. *This* apple, *this* book, *this* chair are each a holy thing, made and sustained by God and by his cocreators. *This* person to whom I am talking is a manifestation of the image of God. *This* moment of time is a *kairos* moment; that is, a moment filled with the presence of God. Indeed, as Orthodox bishop Kallistos Ware says, "The whole universe is a cosmic Burning Bush, filled with the divine Fire yet not consumed."[8]

45

In the last chapter we saw how this power is able to even use weakness to do its bidding. Here we see that the power that at one level is alien—that is, exists outside of us and comes to us—is also a power that reverberates through every thing and every moment of our existence. This divine attribute is not merely wielded from a distant spiritual reality called heaven but energizes every molecule of our existence.

We have noted how the psalmist put it:

> Where shall I go from your Spirit?
> Or where shall I flee from your presence?
> If I ascend to heaven, you are there!
> If I make my bed in Sheol, you are there!
> If I take the wings of the morning
> and dwell in the uttermost parts of the sea,
> even there your hand shall lead me,
> and your right hand shall hold me.
>
> Psalm 139:7–10

Sometimes it's clear how that right hand upholds and sustains us and all that is. And sometimes it's incognito. But it is there, like the energy that quietly and anonymously fills our homes with warmth and light and so many good things.

4

All-Knowing Grace (Omniscient)

Even before a word is on my tongue,
 behold, O LORD, you know it altogether.
You hem me in, behind and before.

Psalm 139:4–5

My wife, Barbara, and I have been married for over thirty years, and yet some corners of our inner lives remain dark to each another. We know a lot about one another. A lot. But we're still learning how to reveal some secrets. It's still scary after all these years.

Think of other relationships, and it becomes clear how much we hide from others. Most of the time, we're trying to make a good impression: on our boss, on our co-workers, on our neighbors, on the stranger for whom we open the door at the bank. We share some intimacies with friends, lovers, parents, children, priests, and pastors—but we do not tell everything to anyone.

We hold back in wisdom—it's probably not a good idea to be telling co-workers of the opposite sex about your temptations to lust. It's not wise for parents to tell their young children how they sometimes wish they didn't have children.

But we also hold back in fear. What would he think if I told him how hateful I sometimes feel? Would she still speak to me if I admitted my addiction to pornography? Could I still work in the church if they knew how many doubts I have?

Would I be accepted if I told all? We long to be in the company of someone who will not blink no matter what we say. But we don't believe this is possible in this world. We've all endured humiliation when a confidant shared one of our secrets to another. We live daily with a low-grade fear that somebody is going to find out something about us we do not wish to reveal.

Bringing God into the picture does not seem to help. We're told over and over that he accepts us just as we are. But truth be told, we're skeptical. If there is anyone we're really anxious to make a good impression on, it's God.

To be sure, we confess things to God that we confess to no one else. But many confessions are attempts to manipulate the relationship: I admit my greed or selfishness in a moment of contrition. I'm sincere, but I'm also looking for absolution. If I do my part, God will do his part, and all will be well.

I know I'm manipulating God, because while I'm willing to bring some matters before him, I refuse to speak with him about other things. Like the alcoholic who refuses to admit his addiction, I struggle to admit my various addictions. I hide the truth from myself, and in that sense I hide it from God—that is, pretend it's not an issue. Many times when circumstances or a loving rebuke forces me to admit some dark area of my life, I realize I was aware of it for some time—like being aware of the low hum of a speaker while you're listening to a speech; you do not hear that hum if someone is chattering into the microphone, but it becomes obvious when the person stops talking and you just listen.

So while we *say* it's wonderful that God knows everything about us and yet still accepts us, we often don't believe it. If we really believed God accepted us, we wouldn't be hiding these secrets from ourselves and him.

The psalmist does not fall for a cheap piety. Neither does he pretend he can hide something from God. But that doesn't allay his fear:

> O LORD, you have searched me and known me!
>> You know when I sit down and when I rise up;
>>> you discern my thoughts from afar.
>> You search out my path and my lying down
>>> and are acquainted with all my ways.
>> Even before a word is on my tongue,
>>> behold, O LORD, you know it altogether.
>> You hem me in, behind and before.
>
> Psalm 139:1–5

God's knowledge makes him feel trapped. He realizes God will shed light on dark corners of his soul, where secrets of shame, guilt, and doubt huddle in fear. He will have to abandon his attempts at manipulating God. When God does shed light on the psalmist's secrets, he stands before God naked, ashamed, with every dark secret bared.

It is no wonder that the attribute of God's omniscience has fallen on hard times.

When we ponder God's omniscience—his complete knowledge—we can wax eloquent about things philosophical and cosmic. We ask large questions: If God knows everything that is going to happen, does that negate our free will?

If we are truly free to make decisions, does that not mean that God does not really know what we are going to do? And so on.

Important questions to be sure. But in the spiritual life, intellectual doubts often mask an unwillingness to submit oneself to a mysterious yet clear truth.

Current theological discussions of omniscience have made one thing clear: we can no longer hold to an omniscience that comes in the dress of Greek philosophical thought—a rigid, impersonal, and deterministic knowledge where free will is sabotaged. Any talk of omniscience has to be grounded in biblical revelation. And biblical revelation is concerned first and foremost with God's relationship with us.

While no one verse or passage spells out this doctrine in an orderly way, the biblical writers assume God's omniscience. It is one reason God is utterly superior to the gods of other nations. As Isaiah put it:

> Thus says the LORD, the King of Israel
> and his Redeemer, the LORD of hosts:
> "I am the first and I am the last;
> besides me there is no god.
> Who is like me? Let him proclaim it.
> Let him declare and set it before me,
> since I appointed an ancient people.
> Let them declare what is to come, and what will
> happen.
> Fear not, nor be afraid;
> have I not told you from of old and declared it?"
>
> Isaiah 44:6–8

The biblical writers also apply God's omniscience to the depths of the human soul. God knows the secrets of our hearts (see Ps. 44:21), that "the heart is deceitful above all things, and desperately sick" (Jer. 17:9), and that God's knowledge is a form of judgment. As Elihu put it in the book of Job:

> For his eyes are on the ways of a man,
> and he sees all his steps.
> There is no gloom or deep darkness
> where evildoers may hide themselves.
> For God has no need to consider a man further,
> that he should go before God in judgment.
>
> Job 34:21–23

No wonder the psalmist felt hemmed in. The holy God knows the worst about us. How will we survive his scrutiny unscathed by judgment? Theologian Paul Tillich put it like this:

> Our entire inner life, our thoughts and desires, our feelings and imaginations, are known to God. . . . The human resistance against such relentless observation can scarcely be broken. Every psychiatrist and confessor is familiar with the tremendous force of resistance in each personality against even trifling self-revelations. Nobody wants to be known, even when he realizes that his health and salvation depend upon such a knowledge. We do not even wish to be known by ourselves. We try to hide the depths of our souls from our own eyes. We refuse to be our own witness. How then can we stand the mirror in which nothing can be hidden?[1]

That's the psalmist's dilemma—and ours.

The very thing that makes us feel trapped is the very thing that also reveals God's grace. If we can muster the courage to allow God's omniscience to judge us, we will see that before and after the righteous judgment, there has been the omniscience of grace.

The autumn after my thirteenth birthday, my mother and brother and I began attending a fundamentalist church at which the pastor gave an altar call every week, if not for conversion, then for recommitment. He was a master at his craft, and every week I felt guilty when he began warming up to the altar call. Week after week, this part of the service became increasingly oppressive. As December rolled around, I decided that I didn't want to celebrate Christmas with this guilt hanging over me. So the Sunday before Christmas when the pastor told the congregation to bow in prayer, and then asked for a show of hands of those who wished to give their lives to Jesus, my hand shot up.

That was usually the end of it, but this week he asked those who had raised hands to come forward to pray with an elder. This was more than I had bargained for, but I was determined to flush the guilt out of my system, so I went forward, and the elder and I went into another room to pray. He led me in a version of the sinner's prayer, and I wept uncontrollably, which we both took as a sign of my true repentance.

The next week I went to church with great expectations. But my joy was crushed when the pastor gave the altar call. Once again, all those feelings of guilt sprang up.

As the months and years unfolded, I slowly understood what had happened. First, the pastor was adept at making people feel guilty, regardless of their moral state. Call it manipulation or prophetic insight into the human condition— it was probably a combination. So the guilt I continued to experience was genuine in some ways and manipulated in others.

Second, I slowly recognized how self-centered my conversion had been. I formally "accepted Jesus as my Lord and Savior," and I confessed my sins as a prelude to that. But in fact, what I really wanted was to eliminate guilt. I wanted to stop feeling uncomfortable. And I was trying to use God to make that happen.

Third, I realized that God knew this about me when I walked forward on the December morning. He knew I had little intention of making Jesus my Lord at that moment; he knew I was very much still lord of my life, trying to shape it according to my understanding of happiness.

God in his foreknowledge knew that when he drew me into his family, I would lust and lie and gossip and slander and practice all manner of immorality in the years ahead. He knew the particular sins and the particular people I would sin against. He has known for some time the evil inclination I recognized for the first time yesterday in worship. He knows this morning how I'm going to fail him before the morning is out.

And yet, despite his complete knowledge of my dark heart and my wicked future, he accepted my initial sinner's prayer. He has remained committed to me despite his full knowledge of my deeds, words, and motives; past, present, and future. As Paul put it: "if we are faithless, he remains faithful—for he cannot deny himself" (2 Tim. 2:13).

Like exploring a dark cave with a small flashlight, we discover the contours of this grace only slowly. Once in a while, we come upon a huge cavern of mercy, where the stalactites and stalagmites of grace overwhelm us with their beauty. We realize that this grace has been dripping into our lives for years, creating something beautiful when we thought there was only darkness.

We have the courage to explore this cave now, because we learn that only in the darkness will we discover the beauty of God's grace.

Omniscience then is not so much a theological attribute or a philosophical problem as it is a revelation of God's mercy. It will indeed inspire fear when we first start reflecting on it. Just ask the psalmist. But the fear of the Lord is also the beginning of wisdom and grace.

5

The Presence
of the Forsaken
(Omnipresent)

Cast me not away from your presence, and take not
your Holy Spirit from me.

Psalm 51:11

L ike most people, I want to know God's presence. I
pray for it. I ponder how to open myself more to it. I
have fleeting moments when I think that happens. I even get
spiritually greedy and wonder if it is possible to "practice the
presence" all day long.

I sometimes wonder, though, if I know what I am asking for.
Because those in the Bible who seemed to enjoy a favorable
relationship with God were nonetheless sometimes desperate
to avoid God. Take Adam and Eve.

After the blessed couple had disobeyed the command of
God, they intuitively sense something tragic has occurred.

They are rightly afraid of God and want to escape him: "And they heard the sound of the LORD God walking in the garden in the cool of the day, and the man and his wife hid themselves from the presence of the LORD God among the trees of the garden" (Gen. 3:8).

Later biblical writers note that along with the desire to run from God's holy presence comes the knowledge of the impossibility of escaping it. At one point the prophet Amos heard the Lord speak these alarming words:

> Strike the capitals until the thresholds shake,
>   and shatter them on the heads of all the people;
> and those who are left of them I will kill with the
>   sword;
>   not one of them shall flee away;
>   not one of them shall escape.
> If they dig into Sheol,
>   from there shall my hand take them;
> if they climb up to heaven,
>   from there I will bring them down.
> If they hide themselves on the top of Carmel,
>   from there I will search them out and take them;
> and if they hide from my sight at the bottom of the
>   sea,
>   there I will command the serpent, and it shall
>   bite them.
>
> Amos 9:1–3

Such presence is not something a sane person prays for. This suggests something about my prayers: I may not be as sane as I imagine. I may not be as in touch with reality as I think. Likely I am not aware of the darkness of my guilt nor the blinding righteousness of God. I think of God's presence as if it amounted to walking on an open beach, basking in the sunshine that warms me through and through. Instead, the reality is more like a prison courtyard at night, with God as the glaring searchlight following my every step.

My walk-in-the-sunshine fantasy world is a defense mechanism. I had a friend who used to smile and giggle whenever she talked about fearful things, because she couldn't bring herself to face her fears. Laughter, false bravado, and mindless diversion are common ways to defend oneself against the reality of God's holy presence. Another way is religion.

Adam and Eve tried to hide from God "among the trees of the garden" (Gen. 3:8), in the midst of Paradise itself. Religious life can easily become an attempt to medicate our guilt and handcuff the wrath of God. We formally acknowledge a few shortcomings, and God is obligated to avert his holy gaze. That's how we spell relief—by getting God to stop thinking about us. In this and other ways, the devoutly religious life can easily become a way to avoid the presence of God.

This is one of the chief complaints of the Hebrew prophets and of Jesus. They saw people could be extraordinarily precise about ritual sacrifice and the details of a religious life. To measure and manage their religion, they had dumbed down the commandments of God so that religion was more user-friendly; it made Yahweh accessible to the average churchgoing Harry. Naturally, it became easier to conclude that they had done what was required of them. They imagined they had convinced God that he could leave them well enough alone now, that he could take his presence elsewhere, judging other sinners of other nations, for example.

On the one hand, we realize that to meet such a God can only result in our death: "For man shall not see me and live," says God to Moses (Exod. 33:20). On the other hand, we know that we cannot live without God: "Cast me not away from your presence," pleads David, "and take not your Holy Spirit from me" (Ps. 51:11).

What prevents the consuming fire from consuming us is repentance. Like a fire protection suit, it shields us from the flames of judgment. David knows it is not religion and ritual as such that protect us:

> For you will not delight in sacrifice, or I would
>   give it;
> you will not be pleased with a burnt offering.
> The sacrifices of God are a broken spirit;
>   a broken and contrite heart, O God, you will
>   not despise.

Psalm 51:16–17

The paradox is that those who think they deserve to be in God's presence are those who don't, and those who recognize they don't belong in God's presence are invited to enter it. This is the point of many of Jesus's parables. In one, a Pharisee is proud of his religious life and boldly enters the temple to pray; a publican is hesitant to even approach the temple because of his sin. And yet it is the publican who enjoys God's favor.

Most of us fall somewhere between these two extremes. We're not self-righteous enough to assume we can enter God's temple. But neither are we particularly contrite—or even sufficiently aware of our sins to know we have no business being there. Instead we calmly walk up, knock at the temple door, and ask to be let in—"O God, show me your presence." We don't come proclaiming our righteousness, but we do play on a sense of cosmic fairness: God loves everyone; I'm not perfect, but I'm no better or worse than the next person; why shouldn't I enjoy God's loving presence? Besides, he knows I need him to get through this life, so he really should help me out here.

When God doesn't show himself, we are apt to fall into self-pity; we complain about God's unfairness and how hard he makes our lives. We may even abandon the faith because it "doesn't work."

The key to turning this around is to let the searing spotlight of God do its work. It means honestly facing our shortcomings, weaknesses, flaws, and addictions. It means admitting that despite the many genetic and cultural influences swaying us, in the end we are responsible for our calcified hearts and our wayward lives.

Such contrition dims the blinding spotlight and breaks down the prison walls so that we suddenly find ourselves in the open field of grace with the rays of love penetrating us through and through. Paradoxically, the reason the prison walls collapse is that we know we do not deserve to be free.

Such repentance is painful, hard work. It is, in fact, impossible work. No person has the strength or wisdom to face their darkness. We rightly suspect that coming face-to-face with the reality of this darkness is another sure path to death.

But of course Jesus Christ is walking with us, the one who has gone ahead of us and trudged the path of sin and darkness on the cross. He knows our complete depravity; he knows how black the darkness is within us. And he wants to lead us to the place he has already been.

That's repentance. It is not our solitary work of unearthing the disgusting within us. It is Jesus Christ leading us through the dark places where he has already been so that his light can heal us. He is not surprised by anything he sees. He has seen it all before we have, and nonetheless he wills to lead us on this spiritual journey.

What we eventually discover, and must rediscover throughout the life of faith, is that the judging presence of God, from which we hide, and the dark reality of our sin, which we deny, are both signs of God's gracious presence. Grace does not always feel good, certainly not at the beginning of the journey of repentance. But is it grace nonetheless, because it is a sign of God's presence.

You would think that once we grasp this, all would be well. But there is another way in which grace is no escape from the unnerving presence of God. In some ways, the more we know God, the more it makes things worse.

Let's revisit the story of Jonah. He receives an extraordinary grace—a clear and specific call on his life. How many of us wish for such divine guidance? How many of us plead that God would clearly make his will for us known? We yearn to have purpose, direction, and meaning in our lives, and here is Jonah getting our wish.

And he wants nothing of it, so he flees "from the presence of the LORD" (Jonah 1:3). He goes in the opposite direction to avoid the unmistakable call of God on his life. The Jonah reflex, unfortunately, is something we all suffer from.

A friend sensed an unmistakable call to bring his lust under the control of the Spirit. The thought of giving up this pleasure so frightened him, he immediately plunged into an orgy of porn.

Another friend had this nagging sense she was to create a midweek service for the church, so she spent the next two years volunteering for so many things in the parish that she had little time to plan such a service.

I never cease to be amazed at how often I receive an unmistakable divine reminder that I am to give myself to the ministry of writing. And how often I also find my life filled with countless projects—all of which I happily signed up for—which squeeze writing time out.

Why do we avoid the call of God on our lives? I know that the more I give myself to that call, the more I must crucify the self. The more I do that, the more I meet Jesus the crucified, and that is indeed a mercy. But in that meeting, I am always called to a deep crucifixion. No thanks, I say. And so I flee the call of God, and run from the presence of the Lord.

Again, my prayers for the presence of God may be formally good—better than praying for God to go away, I suppose. But in reality, I live my life as if I were praying that God would go away and stay away. I manage things quite well without him, and I'm more than a bit peeved when he shows up and interrupts my life.

I think if we're honest, we have to admit we have no use for God's omnipresence. Some create elaborate philosophical reasons why the classical doctrine no longer makes sense in a postmodern age. Others bitterly complain about the apparent absence of God. But I suspect the reality is that most of us prefer it this way. In addition to being able to manage our lives without interference, we also get the self-pitying pleasure of complaining about God's absence and, as a result, how life is so lonely and meaningless!

The good news is that God knows all this because, whether we deny it or not, he is always present. As the prophet Jeremiah put it, "Am I a God at hand, declares the LORD, and not a God far away? Can a man hide himself in secret places so that I cannot see him? declares the LORD. Do I not fill heaven and earth? declares the LORD" (Jer. 23:23–24).

And as he hounded Jonah and hunted down Adam and Eve, he will not let us forget his abiding presence.

Most of the time, that is. Sometimes God gives us the distinct impression that he is nowhere to be found.

At such times we doubt ourselves. We wonder what we've done wrong. Which of our sins has blocked our ears to heaven's voice? We repent, we pray, we plead for God to make himself present in some small way. Even if we will end up dodging him, we still want some sense that we're not alone in the universe.

At such times we doubt God; it suddenly occurs to us that all this God-talk we've engaged in for decades may have been a lie. All those times when we felt an extraordinary presence, well, it must have been brain chemicals. Then we feel more alone than ever.

But in fact, we are in very good company. The likes of Martin Luther, Saint John of the Cross, and Mother Teresa—those who knew special intimacy with God—experienced long periods when God was nowhere to be found. "Jesus has a very special love for you," Mother Teresa wrote her confessor in 1979. "As for me, the silence and the emptiness is so great that I look and do not see, listen and do not hear."[1]

The attribute of omnipresence helps us understand what is going on at such times. It reminds us that despite our feeling that God is absent, he remains present. An omnipresent God cannot help but be present!

This helps us realize that the omnipresent God must deliberately be withdrawing a sense of his presence. Sometimes that is due to some grievous word or deed that we're called to confess. Sometimes it may mean we're being asked to live ever more deeply by faith and not sight. But I believe that mostly God withdraws a sense of his presence so that we can become more like Jesus, more like God himself.

As paradoxical as it may seem, Jesus experienced this absence on the cross, so much so that he cried out, "My God, my God, why have you forsaken me?" (Mark 15:34). As one who was fully human, he realized the frightening chasm that lies between a holy, infinite God and a sinful, finite people.

Jesus's experience of forsakenness also harkens to the forsakenness God has endured. As the Lord spoke through the prophet Hosea:

> When Israel was a child, I loved him,
>   and out of Egypt I called my son.
> The more they were called,
>   the more they went away;
> they kept sacrificing to the Baals
>   and burning offerings to idols.
>
> Hosea 11:1–2

When we experience forsakenness, we are experiencing in some small way what God experiences when we abandon him (if we can speak this way, for an immutable God does not experience as we experience). When we experience forsakenness, we experience something akin to Christ's sense of abandonment on the cross. When we experience forsakenness, we are participating in the very life of God the Father and of Jesus Christ his Son.

We tend to think that the deeper we immerse ourselves into the life of God, the more bliss we will know. Indeed—and thank God for such bliss! But the clear testimony of Scripture, both Old and New Testaments, reveals that forsakenness— a sense of abandonment by the one whose love you most need—is part and parcel of the life of God in Christ. When God withdraws his sensible presence, he is allowing us to experience something of the divine life.

This is part of the way God makes us perfect as he is perfect. And it is also the reason we can truly love others. As Paul put it, "For as we share abundantly in Christ's sufferings, so through Christ we share abundantly in comfort too. If we are afflicted, it is for your comfort and salvation" (2 Cor. 1:5–6). To know the hopelessness of spiritual loneliness is to enter into the heart of suffering. It is only in this way that we can truly comfort anyone who suffers—offering not words from above but an arm from the side, not wisdom that stands apart from pain but tears that weep with it.

The spiritual struggles of Mother Teresa came as a shock to the world. People were amazed not only that she had long periods where God's absence was a torture, but that she could still minister to the poorest of the poor. What we fail to appreciate is that the experience of spiritual loneliness was what enabled Mother Teresa to truly love and comfort those who themselves felt abandoned by God and man.

In such moments—when the forsaken comfort one another—the presence of God is made known in new ways. Where two or three are gathered in his name, Jesus says, there he is. That's when, as Paul said, we share abundantly in the comfort only God's presence can bring.

PART 2

Biblical Attributes

6

The Everlasting Now
(Eternal)

> And this is eternal life, that they know you the only
> true God, and Jesus Christ whom you have sent.
>
> John 17:3

On the surface, it seems like wonderful news that the prophet Isaiah announces: "Have you not known? Have you not heard? The LORD is the everlasting God, the Creator of the ends of the earth" (Isa. 40:28).

He explains:

> He does not faint or grow weary;
>   his understanding is unsearchable.
> He gives power to the faint,
>   and to him who has no might he increases strength.
> Even youths shall faint and be weary,
>   and young men shall fall exhausted;

but they who wait for the LORD shall renew their
   strength;
they shall mount up with wings like eagles;
they shall run and not be weary;
they shall walk and not faint.

                                              Isaiah 40:28–31

We have an everlasting God, who is not subject to the
limitations of the human body. Our fatigue at each day's end
reminds us of the weariness we'll know at life's end, and our
sleep points to the final rest to which we all are destined. Since
God is everlasting, since he does not grow weary and die, says
Isaiah, he is a source of vitality for us, the weary and dying.

Many of the faithful have known this reality. We hear stories—some of which we tell about ourselves—about moments
when strength seemed at its very end, when grief or despair
robbed us of hope, when getting out of bed each morning, let
alone attending to the myriad of daily responsibilities awaiting
us, seemed to require a will of heroic proportions.

Yet through prayer, suddenly or slowly one discovers a
new vitality, at least enough to take the next step, and then
the next. We know this did not come from within, from some
hidden or newly discovered but previously untapped reser-
voir; instead we sense it came to us from outside ourselves.
We did not faint but walked; we did not grow weary but ran;
we did not fall exhausted but felt at times as if we soared like
an eagle. We know it as the gift of the everlasting God, who
does not grow weary or die.

The good news of an everlasting God also starkly contrasts
with our experience of this transitory life. Everything we cherish is passing away. We try not to dwell on this frightening
reality, but when we do, we're tempted to grasp ever more
desperately that which we cherish, even to the point of idolatry. This is the benevolent side of idolatry; it's not merely
an attempt to replace almighty God with a lesser god but is
driven by a fear of losing a gift of God.

But to know an everlasting God is to know that nothing truly good will ever pass away. It is to know freedom from anxiety and despair. That which we cherish—from the fellowship of family and friends to the simple pleasures of drink and food and everything between—may pass away in one form, but the promise is that a new heaven and earth will recreate them in a way that time cannot destroy.

It is indeed a blessing to know an everlasting God. But it is also a curse.

The curse is revealed in the popular humor that is associated with "eternal life." The thought of strumming a harp on a bed of clouds or worshiping with the 144,000 hour after hour, year after year, century after century elicits appropriate wisecracks about boredom. We jest about unending and unaltered goodness, saying we'd find more happiness in hell with "worldly" friends, who at least know how to have a good time.

Such lighthearted remarks point to a genuine concern that an everlastingly perfect life—the promise of heaven—might be a type of hell, for among the many things that make life interesting are its beginnings and ends.

The prospect of embarking on a new relationship or intellectual interest or diversion or social cause prompts us to hop out of bed in the mornings and pursue the day with vigor. Conversely, we know times when ending a good thing seems "meet and right." Relationships run their course, intellectual interests flag, diversions bore, and our pet solutions for a social problem no longer seem adequate. Endings are often imbued with poignancy when we ponder what could or should have been, but even poignancy has a certain sweetness attached to it.

Can we imagine an attractive form of life without beginnings and ends? It's hard. A life that goes on and on in everlasting bliss does not engage the imagination. It feels like a curse. Yet despite our attempts to edit this idea of "eternal life" with a more sophisticated image of the new heavens and the new earth, a part of us continues to doubt the attraction of everlasting life with an everlasting God.

A second curse of knowing an everlasting God comes when we ponder the length of our years. If, as Isaiah notes, the nations, in comparison to God, are "like a drop from a bucket, and are accounted as the dust on the scales" (Isa. 40:15), how much more individuals? "It is [God] who sits above the circle of the earth, and its inhabitants are like grasshoppers" (Isa. 40:22), Isaiah says, though he might have said mayflies.

These insects, mayflies, have a technical name: *ephemeridae*, which is Latin for "lives but a day." This refers to the very last stage of their lives. A mayfly begins as an egg (one to three weeks), moves on to nymph (eleven to twenty-four months), then dun (one to four days), and then spinner. At each stage these insects are subject to predators—mostly fish, who comb the waters seeking prey. But it is the last stage—the adult, mature stage—that is an image of futility. These spinners emerge from their last molt finally ready to sexually reproduce. After laying their eggs, they fall exhausted on the water, where hungry trout devour them.

When a mayfly hatch occurs, the river looks like a fog of insects, with millions emerging and mating and dying and being consumed in a day's time. In this case, it is man who sits above the bank of the river, and the surrounding inhabitants are but mayflies, so many they cannot be named, so ephemeral that each dies unknown.

When we compare our lives with that of an everlasting God, is not our span of three score years and ten less than a mayfly day? If we ponder the millions of human lives that wander this earth and mate and perish, all seemingly in a day, can we really believe that an everlasting God notices and cares? The existence of an everlasting God merely mocks the shortness of our lives.

The curse of knowing an everlasting God is made worse when we ponder the difference between the words *everlasting* and *eternal*. In most instances, they are synonyms in the Bible and in our conversation, both suggesting the unending stretch of time. But *eternal* is a word that also points beyond time.

Time is brought into existence by the Creator: "And God said, 'Let there be lights in the expanse of the heavens to separate the day from the night. And let them be for signs and for seasons, and for days and years'" (Gen. 1:14). To say that God is everlasting is to talk about him from the perspective of time. Within the confines of time, nothing more wonderful can be said about God than that he spans the entire length of time.

But God is not confined by time. He stands above it, as it were, looking down on the timeline of our history. Thus his ability to know the future and the past as if they were the present. This is the other dimension of God's being *eternal*: he transcends time.

This perspective may answer questions we have about divine knowledge—e.g., how does God know the future? But while answering one question, it creates another: if God stands above time, is he truly connected to it? And if he is not—as this aspect of eternity suggests—then is he really connected to his creation, to his people, to me?

We are left with a grand God, whose transcendence makes us marvel but whose distance from us cannot be bridged. We are left alone in the galaxy, with a God who watches the human mayfly hatch from another part of the cosmos, as millions of us rise from the waters, mate, and die before the sun sets. We have as much possibility of reaching God as a mayfly does of flying to the moon.

It is no wonder that this aspect of God's eternity is questioned by some. Philosopher and theologian Grace Jantzen put it like this: "A timeless and immutable God could not be personal, because he could not create or respond, perceive or act, think, remember, or do any of the other things persons do which require time."[1]

Some even argue that God is metaphysically constrained by time: "God's concrete nature participates in the life of the universe and is affected by it," says David Miller. "God suffers, enjoys, and changes. So God affects history and is affected by the joys and sufferings of humankind."[2] It's not just that an eternal God mysteriously but graciously decided to live with us in the constraints of time—that seems to be the biblical idea—but that God is no longer eternal or transcendent in any meaningful sense. Furthermore, for us to identify with him, he must be as constrained by time as we are. Some now relegate the idea of God's eternity to being another of those doctrines that arise less from the Bible and more from Greek philosophy.

On main street, the reaction is similar. We've put this attribute in theological storage. It seems irrelevant or uninteresting to those raised in a culture of intimacy, where the meaning of life is bound up with personal relationships. It may be a grand idea that God is eternal, but it simply doesn't scratch our existential itch for a God who "is affected by the joys and sufferings of humankind." In fact, the idea of "the eternity of God" makes us break out in boredom.

And yet biblical revelation will not abandon the word *eternal*, even using it in a world dominated by Greek philosophical thought. And it is used in a way that suggests that rather than *eternal* driving a wedge between us and God, it actually becomes the bridge between us: "And this is eternal life, that they know you the only true God, and Jesus Christ whom you have sent" (John 17:3).

This is a crucial theme in the Gospel of John. As New Testament theologian George Eldon Ladd put it, "The expressed purpose for the writing of the Fourth Gospel is that its readers may know the way to eternal life through faith in Jesus Messiah (John 20:31). The purpose of Jesus's coming into the world was that people might enjoy this type of life

(John 10:10). . . . Furthermore, the primary emphasis in John is upon eternal life as a present experience."[3]

John says that the very aspect of God that makes him seem remote and unreachable—his eternity—has in fact become near and intimate in Jesus Christ.

This works itself out in two ways. It is commonly said that to show love, one must spend quality time with another. Though I might rack up hours of time with someone sitting right next to me—let's say, on a plane—no one would call this an act of love.

At the same time, neither does spending merely five minutes a day of focused conversation with my wife constitute love. The fuller truth is that love requires both a sense of quality and a span of quantity.

Jesus Christ offers us both.

When the Gospel writer John talks about eternal life, a lot of the time he's talking about the quality of life offered in Christ. He quotes Jesus as saying, "I came that they may have life and have it abundantly" (John 10:10). Abundant life is a synonym for eternal life, and eternal life is to know God and Jesus Christ. To experience eternal life is to experience a remarkable quality of life, an experience so intense that one loses track of time. It is such a rich reveling in the moment that it's as if the past and future collapse into an everlasting present.

God in his profligate grace gives everyone a taste of such life in the most mundane of activities. Computer hobbyists commonly know "eternal life" when they give themselves to solving a program glitch. The problem can absorb them, so that they start working on it right after dinner, and when they next lift their heads, they look out the window and see the sun peeking above the horizon. They marvel because they have had no sense of the passing of time, so intense was the activity in which they were engaged.

Lovers commonly know the experience of transcending time, from getting lost in conversation to the ecstasy of physical union. As Shakespeare's Cleopatra rehearses to Mark Antony, "Eternity was in our lips and eyes, / Bliss in our brows' bent."[4]

Indeed, "[God] has planted eternity in the human heart" (Eccles. 3:10 NLT), and such common experiences are a merciful glimpse into the very life of God, which has been most deeply experienced by the mystics. Saint John of the Cross describes one such experience that led to the writing of his famous book, saying,

> I remained lost in oblivion;
> My face I reclined on the Beloved;
> All ceased and I abandoned myself,
> Leaving my cares forgotten among the lilies.[5]

Between ecstasy and the mundane is where most of us meet Christ so as to know, even briefly, abundant life: in the Eucharist, in the reading of Scripture, in prayer. It often happens when we are so engrossed in serving others, so embedded in the joy of love, that when we're done, we wonder where the time went, and we know that in serving the "least of these" (Matt. 25:40), we have been in the presence of the Eternal One.

Such moments come and go in the spiritual life. They are the product of both spiritual intensity and divine grace. In some periods, they come almost predictably: I have known seasons of prayer in which every morning eternity was to be had by simply stilling my mind. In other seasons, we are called to live by faith—and to prepare for those seasons when time seems to be no more.

In the end, of course, when it comes to God's love, little separates *everlasting* and *eternal*. If divine love is experienced with an intensity that transcends time, making every moment an eternal present, then it is also true that we will experience this love in an unending stretch of time in the new heaven and earth: "I am the resurrection and the life," says Jesus.

"Whoever believes in me, though he die, yet shall he live, and everyone who lives and believes in me shall never die" (John 11:25–26).

That love, as best we can humanly imagine it, will include times of gazing into our Lover's eyes, of joyful play in the fields of delight, of animated conversations with friends, of meaningful work in the new Jerusalem.

This eternity is a concrete reality, one in which resurrected, bodily creatures live in space and time, where they know both the joy of change, of beginnings and endings, as well as the love that never leaves nor forsakes.

It is finally a mystery how transcendent Eternity can become immanent in the severe confines of human life, but such is the nature of the Good News we are invited to live.

7

Liberating Love (Lord)

When one turns to the Lord, the veil is removed. Now the Lord is the Spirit, and where the Spirit of the Lord is, there is freedom.

2 Corinthians 3:16–17

On a brisk November day in 1202, Assisi's militia, both knights on horse and soldiers on foot, marched through the city's streets. The townsfolk cheered as the troops filed out the city gates, down the gradual slope upon which Assisi sits, to the plain that spreads out below the town. At the same hour, soldiers of rival Perugia were also marching toward the plain, and by midmorning the two armies stared at each other a half-mile apart.

Then Perugia charged. The plain sounded with the thunder of hooves and the shouts of men bracing themselves for the first blows of battle. The fighting raged for hours, but for Assisi, as one contemporary historian noted, "The final defeat came very late, but the slaughter was very severe."[1] Those who were not killed were taken prisoner.

That included one of Assisi's elite company, *Compagnia dei Cavaliera*, and a wealthy merchant's young son named Francis. Francis, like most young men of his day, had memorized the songs of the troubadours, ballads of knights and ladies and the glory of battle. But now it all didn't look so glorious. He found himself bound in chains, dragged to Perugia, and thrown into a dungeon prison. The dungeon was lit by only a few torches, which did nothing to alleviate the dampness nor the smell of men's sweat, rotting hay, and human waste.

For a while Francis remained upbeat and went about cheering up the other soldiers with self-mocking jokes about his chains. But the miserable conditions—and especially the absence of family and friends—took their toll. Francis had a deserved reputation as an extrovert. He loved company, and whenever friends were looking for a good time, they turned to Francis to ask, "What should we do tonight?" Prison ended not only Francis's freedom but his friendships, and that, I believe, took the greater toll. By the time his father was able to negotiate Francis's release (which took about a year), Francis had become ill and had settled into a quiet depression.[2]

This early episode in the life of Francis of Assisi is little known, but it shaped him deeply. I note it here because it has always seemed to me like a metaphor for the spiritual life. A part of us wants to do great deeds for God, to wage glorious battle, to win victory over enemies, whether those enemies are social injustice or personal sin. But more often than not, we find ourselves defeated and, more importantly, imprisoned in the darkness of despair. It isn't the defeat that's the problem—we're used to losing and then picking ourselves up to fight new battles. That's just the rhythm of life.

What gets to us is the separation from love. For Francis, it was the absence of family and friends; for us, it sometimes feels like alienation from God. It seems like we're on the other side of an expansive plain and, for reasons beyond our control, separated from God, held captive by an enemy whose power seems unbroken.

Catholic writer Ronald Rolheiser says the same thing with another metaphor:

> There is within us a fundamental dis-ease, an unquenchable fire that renders us incapable, in this life, of ever coming to full peace. This desire lies at the center of our lives, the marrow of our bones, and in the deep recesses of the soul. We are not easeful human beings who occasionally get restless, serene persons who once in awhile are obsessed by desire. The reverse is true. We are driven persons, forever obsessed, congenitally diseased, living lives, as Thoreau suggested, of quiet desperation.[3]

And our lives remain restless, as Augustine said, until we find our rest in God.[4]

While we instinctively long for union with God, we are presented with a God who, more often than not, describes himself as *Lord*. This term seems to put God over us, even against us. He is master; we are servants. He commands; we obey. The Lord is king and sovereign, a being we approach as the Scarecrow, the Tin Man, and the Lion approached the Wizard of Oz—in fear and with trembling.

While *Lord* has become a term of intimacy in some Christian circles, modern feminist scholars have seen most acutely the biblical and theological essence of the term, one that seems to push God away. Rosemary Radford Ruether, for example, says that the phrase "Christ is Lord" is fundamentally an imperial term parallel to "Caesar is Lord." This is the context in which the Nicene Creed talks about Jesus ("I believe . . . in Jesus Christ, our Lord"). This creed, she argues, fuses a twin heritage: that of the Hebrew prophets and Greek philosophy.[5]

In Zechariah, the Messiah is described as a warrior-king who will overthrow enemy empires and install Israel in power.

Enemy nations will be reduced to client states who will come to Jerusalem and pay tribute to the new ruling empire. To this notion, Ruether says, was added the concept of the divine *Logos*, or *Nous* ("mind") of God, who in Greek thought is the means through which the universe is governed. This in turn led to the idea that all of creation is ordered in a hierarchical "chain of Being": "Just as the Nous of God governs nature, so the Greeks must govern barbarians, masters govern slaves and men govern women. The free Greek male is seen as the natural aristocrat, representing mind and headship in nature."[6]

Thus in early church theology, Ruether says, "Christ becomes the *Pantocrator*, the cosmic governor of a new Christianized universal empire. The Christian emperor, with the Christian bishop at his right hand, becomes the new Vicar of Christ on earth, governing the Christian state of the new redeemed order of history."[7]

This does not sound like a faith where sitting around a campfire holding hands singing "Kum Ba Yah" is the defining characteristic. Ruether uses this historical analysis to condemn the Christianity that emerged, but this history cuts more ways than she imagines.

The church construed reality this way precisely because it needed to remember its place in the Roman Empire. Nicene theology announced that the church was not one religion among others, let alone a sorrowful persecuted minority. Instead, it was the advanced guard of a great Lord, who rules the universe and would come again to establish his just kingdom.

As such, Nicene theology remains a crucial—I'd argue the most crucial—framing of the faith. The Nicene Creed reminds us to whom we owe ultimate allegiance, and that God in Jesus Christ through the Holy Spirit—not the state, not the culture, not some ideology—controls our destiny.

And while it appears that highlighting the authority of the Lord God sabotages a close and vital relationship with him, the opposite proves to be the case.

This apparent contradiction, like many of the other paradoxes of God's attributes, is grounded in something deeper and more profound than mere historical usage. The biblical account suggests that the rupture between God and man is not only historical but cosmic in scope. The biblical writers have to resort to metaphorical language to describe that break, and one early image—and one pervasive in the early church—was that of captivity. The human condition is likened to imprisonment: we are held by enemy forces, separated from our Creator. We are wasting away in the dungeon of alienation, sin, and death—not unlike Francis in the Perugian prison. The reason we cannot enjoy God is not because of God's sovereign status but because of the human condition.

This chasm is not easily breached, and to do so in fact requires extraordinary power; the chains of bondage must be broken by a greater force. As the apostle Paul put it:

> For as in Adam all die, so also in Christ shall all be made alive. But each in his own order: Christ the firstfruits, then at his coming those who belong to Christ. Then comes the end, when he delivers the kingdom to God the Father after destroying every rule and every authority and power.
>
> 1 Corinthians 15:22–24

Paul reverts to this imagery of liberation time and again in his writing: "The creation itself will be set free from its bondage to decay and obtain the freedom of the glory of the children of God" (Rom. 8:21).

Theologian Gustav Aulen says this was the primary understanding of the early church: "The work of Christ is first and foremost a victory over the powers which hold mankind in bondage: sin, death, and the devil."[8]

This is ultimately a future event, when our relationship with God will be known without the confines and ambiguity of history. But even now we know the firstfruits: "God's love has been poured into our hearts through the Holy Spirit who has been given to us" (Rom. 5:5).

That interior reality—our hearts—can now be infused with the very Spirit of God. That is a connection unparalleled in human relationships. Sexual union is a sacrament between man and woman, creating an intimacy that transcends their bodily existence. The relation with God is more intense still, one which Paul summarizes in the most succinct and intimate phrase one can imagine: "Christ *in* you" (Col. 1:27, emphasis added).

In Christ we have been set free from the dungeon—free to once again enjoy the fellowship of the divine family.

And yet there is more to this story. Union with God is not an accomplished fact of our experience. It is a promise; it is the destination of history. In the meantime, we grow in the Spirit. But again, it's "the Lord" that stands at the heart of the transformation.

> When one turns to the Lord, the veil is removed. Now the Lord is the Spirit, and where the Spirit of the Lord is, there is freedom. And we all, with unveiled face, beholding the glory of the Lord, are being transformed into the same image from one degree of glory to another. For this comes from the Lord who is the Spirit.
>
> 2 Corinthians 3:16–18

It is by beholding the cosmic Lord in all his glory—an act that inspires reverence, awe of an "other"—that the veil is removed and the "other" becomes the most intimate of friends.

In fact, the prerequisite of intimacy is separation. We cannot become one with another unless there is an "other" with whom we can become one. There must be two "others" before the two can become one.

The lordship of God is that attribute that announces, as Ruether notes, that God is not us. He is infinite; we are finite. He is omnipotent; we are weak. He controls our destiny; we do not. He is the Sovereign, the Lord. The Other.

As such we can have a genuine relationship with him. We do not become absorbed in the Godhead in a moment of spiritual obliteration. We do not get swallowed up in the divine, being utterly consumed. We enter into a relationship characterized by both reverence and closeness.

Once again, the icon of so much of the spiritual life can help us. Marriage is about the two becoming one, but not in the sense of being absorbed into one another. The man and woman each remain an other, and as an other, they enter into a relationship. The ongoing paradox is that the deeper the relationship, the greater the reverence they have for one another. The more they become familiar to each other, the more they become mysterious.

How much more when we find ourselves in the embrace of God, enjoying a mysterious union with the Lord of the universe in which his sovereignty is an expression of his love—a love that makes itself known in sovereignty.

8

The Weight of Light (Glory)

Blessed be his glorious name forever; may the whole earth be filled with his glory!

Psalm 72:19

What is light?

For a long time, scientists told us light is an electromagnetic wave, which means it is a varying electric and magnetic field.

Sort of. According to quantum physics, light is said to be made up of particles called photons. These carry energy and momentum but have no mass.

Light is one of those things that looks different—wave or particle—depending on how you look at it. But in either case, light is ethereal, vague, lacking definite shape or form. It's not easy to get your head around, let alone your arms.

The Bible often associates the glory of God with light. It begins in the exodus, where God's presence is described as fire.

> Now the appearance of the glory of the LORD was like a devouring fire on the top of the mountain in the sight of the people of Israel. Moses entered the cloud and went up on the mountain. And Moses was on the mountain forty days and forty nights.
>
> Exodus 24:17–18

Or take the vision of Ezekiel, who when overwhelmed with a vision of the divine, resorts to language like this:

> And upward from what had the appearance of his waist I saw as it were gleaming metal, like the appearance of fire enclosed all around. And downward from what had the appearance of his waist I saw as it were the appearance of fire, and there was brightness around him. Like the appearance of the bow that is in the cloud on the day of rain, so was the appearance of the brightness all around.
>
> Such was the appearance of the likeness of the glory of the LORD.
>
> Ezekiel 1:27–28

Similarly, when God becomes flesh, the occasion is accompanied by dazzling light:

> And in the same region there were shepherds out in the field, keeping watch over their flock by night. And an angel of the Lord appeared to them, and the glory of the Lord shone around them, and they were filled with fear.
>
> Luke 2:8–9

So God's glory is radiant light. There is a certain attraction there. But lest we mistake this glory for the warm glow of a spiritual high, we also see how dangerous this light is. God may be a fire, but he is a "devouring fire." The shepherds aren't drawn to the glory of God when they see the heavens lit up, but instead are "filled with fear." They know that this radiant light is capable of killing those who draw near.

Moses was foolish enough to ask to see God's glory, but God in his mercy refused. "You cannot see my face," God replied, "for man shall not see me and live" (Exod. 33:20).

Still, despite its fearsomeness, biblical writers think it is something to celebrate:

> Blessed be the LORD, the God of Israel,
> who alone does wondrous things.
> Blessed be his glorious name forever;
> may the whole earth be filled with his glory!
> Amen and Amen!
>
> Psalm 72:18–19

I appreciate the reverence and enthusiasm of the biblical writers, but only from a distance. For me, like many, "God's glory" is a phrase that remains vague, like the word *light*. I understand that God's glory is real, but like light, I really don't know how or why it "works." Praising it in worship is moving, but what difference does it make day-to-day to know that God is glorious?

We get a hint of another dimension of the word when we realize that the Hebrew word for *glory (kabod)* has overtones of "heaviness" or "weight." This may have made the concept even more confusing for the people of the Old Testament. How can something associated with light have any weight? Wouldn't that require that light take on mass?

In the beginning, says John in chapter 1 of his Gospel, the Word was with God and was God. In him was life and light. And this light "was coming into the world" (v. 9). This Word took on flesh, and as John says, "We have seen his glory, glory as of the only Son from the Father" (v. 14).

This divine glory is, in the end, not the least bit ethereal or vague but heavy and weighty in the most literal sense. This is glory "we looked upon and have touched with our hands" (1 John 1:1). This is a glory that, when we draw near, will not destroy but only give life: "And we all, with unveiled face," wrote Paul, "beholding the glory of the Lord, are being transformed into the same image from one degree of glory to another" (2 Cor. 3:18).

This is a glory that we not only grasp intellectually but can probe physically, like Thomas placing his hand in Jesus's wounds. This is a glory we can get our arms around, like the women who cling to the resurrected Jesus.

Since Jesus—Glory Incarnate—the tangible world has never been the same. Those who look at creation with the eyes of faith will find it infused with glory as never before. For those who know Glory Incarnate, all of creation is imbued with his tangible presence, which means all creation shines with God's glory.[1]

In the book *Love without Limits*, "a monk of the Eastern Church" explains:

> You are looking at the sun? Then think of Him who is the Light of the World, albeit shrouded in darkness. You are looking at the trees and their branches growing green again each spring? Then think of Him who, hanging on the wood of the cross, draws everything to Himself. You are looking at rocks and stones? Then think of the stone in the garden that was blocking the entrance to a tomb. That stone was rolled away and since then the door of the sepulchre has never been shut.[2]

A world freighted with spiritual meaning is not an insight unique to Christian faith, but it finds its fullness there.

Whereas pagan religion wants to deify nature and worship creation, those united with the incarnate Word see creation as a sign that points to the Creator.

It's a circular theophany. The Uncreated has become in Jesus Christ like his creation. In Christ's birth, death, and resurrection, the creation is reclaimed as a sign of the original Garden, and thus it becomes a means of leading us back to God. Maximus the Confessor put it this way:

> He, the undifferentiated, is seen in differentiated things, the simple in the compound. He who has no beginning is seen in things that must have a beginning; the invisible in the visible; the intangible in the tangible. Thus he gathers us together in himself, through every object . . . enabling us to rise into union with him, as he was dispersed in coming down to us.[3]

Once we enjoy this experience, nothing is profane again. Everything becomes holy. Not divine, but holy, set apart for sacred use. Thus everything becomes a means of grace. This is why Saint Benedict wrote in his Rule, "Look upon all the tools and all the property of the monastery as if they were sacred altar vessels."[4]

Thus does God's glory pervade the everyday.

"Faith is the doorway to the mysteries," writes Isaac of Nineveh, an early church father. "What the eyes of the body are for physical objects, faith is for the hidden eyes of the soul. Just as we have two bodily eyes, so we have two spiritual eyes, and each has its own way of seeing. With one we see the glory of God hidden in creatures: with the other we contemplate the glory of God's holy nature when he deigns to give us access to the mysteries."[5]

A story is told about Anthony of the Desert in which a philosopher found him and asked, "Father, how can you be happy when you are deprived of the consolation that books can give?"

Anthony replied, "my philosopher friend, my book is the nature of creatures; and this book is always in front of me when I want to read the words of God."[6]

Some have called the world a "first Bible." Both the Bible and creation not only have the same author but also find their full revelation in Christ, the Logos, the underlying principle of the universe. He confers on creation its deepest meaning—the rhythm of the life, death, and resurrection as revealed by a trinitarian God.

One experience of Saint Benedict brings together these themes of glory and light with the world we inhabit:

> While the disciples were still sleeping, Benedict the man of God was already keeping vigil, anticipating the hour of the night office. Standing in front of his window in the dead of night he was praying to the Lord Almighty when suddenly he saw a light shining, and it dispelled the darkness and sparkled with such brilliance that it would have outshone the light of day. While he was watching it something extraordinary happened. As he described it later, the whole world was gathered up before his eyes as if in a ray of sunlight.[7]

As it turns out, the glory of God is not finally vague and ethereal but is as concrete as the earth beneath our feet. The experience of glory—the radiant light of divinity—gives us not only God but the world that he has made.

9

The Kiss
of Community
(Righteous)

Steadfast love and faithfulness meet;
righteousness and peace kiss each other.

Psalm 85:10

In his early years, whenever Martin Luther read the phrase "the righteousness of God," it terrified him:

That expression "righteousness of God" was like a thunderbolt in my heart. . . . I thought at once that this righteousness was an avenging anger, namely, the wrath of God. I hated Paul with all my heart when I read that the righteousness of God is revealed in the gospel.[1]

He had been steeped in medieval theology, which had taught that divine righteousness was God's active, personal righteousness or justice by which he punishes the unrighteous sinner. So it was only natural that when Luther came across the phrase "the righteousness of God" in Scripture, he balked: "I did not love, yes, I hated the righteous God who punishes sinners."[2]

Today we don't get so worked up over the righteousness of God. Partly we don't really believe God will actually punish people for their sins—it is God's business to forgive, after all! So, contra Luther, we don't spend many sleepless nights worrying about this problem.

That doesn't mean we now *love* the righteousness of God. We're still put off by the idea. All well and good that God is righteous, perfectly good, holy. But when we hear that this God is intent on making us righteous—yikes!

When we hear the word *righteous* in relation to human beings, we mentally think "self-righteous." That's one reason that even though it may be accurate to describe someone as righteous ("morally upright"), we'd hesitate to call them such. It's an adjective that has become associated with the worst sort of religious people, from Pharisees to Puritans. Which leads us back to: why would God want to be associated with such a term?

So we find ourselves once more face-to-face with a classical attribute that does nothing but make God seem more distant. Worse yet, God seems to want to make this an attribute of us!

This word *righteous*, when it refers to people or God, is so subject to misunderstanding that we're going to have to take some time to understand its biblical meaning. That means we're going to have to spend a bit of time rehearsing some biblical theology. For unless we do, we're never going to see how much we actually want to be righteous and how deeply we long for a righteous God.

In the Bible, *righteousness* is not primarily about righteous behavior but more about right standing within a community. Two settings help us understand this word.[3]

In the context of a law court, righteousness refers to the standing of a person in relation to the court's decision. There were no public prosecutors in ancient Hebrew law courts. A plaintiff simply brought suits against a defendant, and a judge decided the case. Righteousness is the status for either party when the court finds in his favor.

I own some apartments, and I once had a tenant who was an alcoholic and was endangering the lives of other tenants (passing out with his stove on) and making himself a nuisance (verbally abusing them when he was drunk). I decided to evict him, but he refused to leave. So we went to court and found ourselves before a judge. The judge read my complaint and decided "for the plaintiff." That is, in the eyes of the court, my tenant was guilty of breaking Illinois law, and I was vindicated. In biblical terms, the judge declared me "righteous."

In biblical times, the standard of judgment was not, naturally, the U.S. Constitution or the laws of the state of Illinois but the covenant law of God as laid out in Exodus, Leviticus, Numbers, and Deuteronomy. Thus *righteousness* became associated not just with right standing before the law court but also with right behavior, that is, behavior that conformed to God's covenant requirements.

In addition, whoever was making the judgment, whether judge or king, not only announced who was righteous but had to be righteous himself—that is, the case had to be tried fairly and in accord with the covenant law, and the judge had to condemn evil and show no partiality ("You shall appoint judges and officers . . . and they shall judge the people with righteous judgment," says Deut. 16:18).

Thus the judgment of that Illinois judge, in biblical parlance, was also "righteous," that is, in accord with the laws of the state of Illinois. We would say the judgment was just or that justice was served. But it's easy to see how in the Old Testament, the word *righteousness* gets closely associated with *justice*.

There is a larger setting still for the word *righteousness*, though it remains closely connected to this first sense. Because the covenant law, the Torah, is the charter for the people of Israel, the word *righteousness* refers to the larger sense that an entire people (not just an individual) can have right standing before the Author of the covenant law.

This sense is best expressed in a famous speech of Moses. He begins by telling the people, "You shall diligently keep the commandments of the LORD your God, and his testimonies and his statutes, which he has commanded you" (Deut. 6:17). We today tend to read this individualistically (as if he was telling individuals to keep the commandments personally), but it's clear that Moses is speaking about the nation here: "And you shall do what is right and good in the sight of the LORD, that it may go well with you, and that you may go in and take possession of the good land that the LORD swore to give to your fathers by thrusting out all your enemies from before you, as the LORD has promised" (Deut. 6:18–19).

Then Moses sums up all that had come to pass—from the slavery in Egypt to the redemption of Israel to the giving of the law. He concludes by reminding the people of their covenantal obligations: "And the LORD commanded us to do all these statutes, to fear the LORD our God, for our good always, that he might preserve us alive, as we are this day. *And it will be righteousness for us, if we are careful to do all this commandment before the LORD our God, as he has commanded us*" (Deut. 6:24–25, emphasis added).

In other words, the *people of Israel* will be considered "righteous" when *as a people* they live faithfully according to the covenant.

Thinking of it from the perspective of the individual, it looks like this: For an individual Israelite to have said he was righteous means more or less the same thing as me saying that I am a citizen of the United States. This doesn't mean that I am a perfect citizen who has never broken the law. It means that I have legal standing in the United States of America; I have certain rights and certain responsibilities. In the same way, a righteous Israelite was not necessarily a person who was morally flawless but one who was counted as a member of the covenant community ultimately ruled by God, with certain rights and responsibilities.

Thinking of it from the perspective of the community, it looks like this: Israel was righteous as a nation when the nation lived according to the covenant of God—that is, when it was recognized by God as his people. Similarly today, a nation is accepted as a legitimate member of the international community when its nationhood is "recognized" by the United Nations. In biblical terms, this nation is "righteous"—that is, it has a legal standing in the international community, with attendant rights and responsibilities. Again, this does not mean that recognized nations obey international law perfectly or practice justice immaculately in their borders. And neither does the fact that Israel was called righteous mean it was perfectly moral. When God declared Israel righteous, he merely recognized the nation as his people.

On the other hand, if the covenant people decided not to accept the responsibilities of covenant life, then they stood before the Judge to endure his just sentence. Thus the opening of Isaiah:

> Hear, O heavens, and give ear, O earth;
>   for the LORD has spoken:
> "Children have I reared and brought up,
>   but they have rebelled against me.
> The ox knows its owner,
>   and the donkey its master's crib,
> but Israel does not know,
>   my people do not understand."
> Ah, sinful nation,
>   a people laden with iniquity,
> offspring of evildoers,

children who deal corruptly!
They have forsaken the LORD,
    they have despised the Holy One of Israel,
    they are utterly estranged.

Isaiah 1:2–4

Religious sacrifice, one part of the covenant law, will not save them if they ignore other parts of the covenant:

When you come to appear before me,
    who has required of you
    this trampling of my courts?
Bring no more vain offerings;
    incense is an abomination to me.
New moon and Sabbath and the calling of
        convocations—
    I cannot endure iniquity and solemn assembly. . . .
Wash yourselves; make yourselves clean;
    remove the evil of your deeds from before my eyes;
cease to do evil,
    learn to do good;
seek justice,
    correct oppression;
bring justice to the fatherless,
    plead the widow's cause.

Isaiah 1:12–13, 16–17

And the consequences of breaking the covenant could not be more devastating:

If you are willing and obedient,
    you shall eat the good of the land;
but if you refuse and rebel,
    you shall be eaten by the sword;
    for the mouth of the LORD has spoken.

Isaiah 1:19–20

The historical stage has become a law court, and Israel stands at the dock, condemned. The people of God are no longer righteous; that is, they have rejected the covenant of God. In one sense, they are no longer the people of God.

Because *righteousness* is directly connected to the covenant law, it is often used as a synonym for moral goodness or for obedience to God's law. Take one example among many:

> The LORD dealt with me according to my
>   righteousness;
>   according to the cleanness of my hands he
>   rewarded me.
> For I have kept the ways of the LORD,
>   and have not wickedly departed from my God.
> For all his rules were before me,
>   and his statutes I did not put away from me.
> I was blameless before him,
>   and I kept myself from my guilt.
> So the LORD has rewarded me according to my
>   righteousness,
>   according to the cleanness of my hands in his
>   sight.
>
> Psalm 18:20–24

But the different meanings slide into one another, and that can easily be confusing. For example, note this verse from the Psalms:

> The LORD judges the peoples;
>   judge me, O LORD, according to my righteousness
>   and according to the integrity that is in me.
>
> Psalm 7:8

Righteousness here can be seen in one light as the equivalent of morally upright behavior. Yet at the same time, the psalmist is calling on God to recognize him as a member of the covenant community: "according to my righteousness" also means "note my citizenship papers!" He has "integrity" in the sense that he is morally sound, yes, but also because who he is and what he does is integrated: he acts like a member of the covenant community because he is a member of the covenant community.

Again, note this passage from Ezekiel:

> If a man is righteous and does what is just and right—if he does not eat upon the mountains or lift up his eyes to the idols of the house of Israel, does not defile his neighbor's wife, . . . commits no robbery, gives his bread to the hungry and covers the naked with a garment, does not lend at interest or take any profit, withholds his hand from injustice, executes true justice between man and man, walks in my statutes, and keeps my rules by acting faithfully—he is righteous; he shall surely live, declares the Lord GOD.
>
> Ezekiel 18:5–9

If *righteous* means merely doing what is right, then the first sentence is a tautology. Of course a righteous person does what is just and right. That's what defines him.

But if *righteous* can mean "one who has standing in the covenant community," that is, a "citizen" of that community, the sentence makes complete sense. As a member of the community, the righteous person has certain responsibilities and privileges: if he lives according the law of the community, he remains a full member of that community, and "he shall surely live" (v. 9).

Note especially the activities described as "just and right"— they are all about relating properly to the King of the community (no idolatry) or about relating properly to the members of the community.

The notion of righteousness in the Old Testament, then, is grounded in relationships, with God and with others. It is about personal morality insofar as that personal morality breaks down a relationship.

These two settings (law court and covenant) combine to produce the theology that was prominent in the Judaism of Jesus's day. To have righteousness meant to belong to the covenant community. Those who belonged to this covenant community agreed to live within the borders of the Torah. They looked to a time when the great and righteous Judge would act in history to vindicate, or "justify," his people, saving them from their enemies—and thus showing the rest of the world they really were God's people.

This understanding is clearly reflected in Matthew. Note Jesus's explanation of the parable of the weeds:

> The field is the world, and the good seed is the sons of the kingdom. The weeds are the sons of the evil one, and the enemy who sowed them is the devil. The harvest is the close of the age, and the reapers are angels. Just as the weeds are gathered and burned with fire, so will it be at the close of the age. The Son of Man will send his angels, and they will gather out of his kingdom all causes of sin and all law-breakers, and throw them into the fiery furnace. In that place there will be weeping and gnashing of teeth. Then the righteous will shine like the sun in the kingdom of their Father.
>
> Matthew 13:38–43

The "good seed" is equated with "the sons of the kingdom," who are called "the righteous"—that is, members of "the kingdom of their Father." These will be vindicated in the great judgment at the end of history.

New Testament writers understood Jesus himself as the quintessential member of the covenant community, one in special relationship with the Father and one who obeys all the covenant obligations. Thus he is referred to as "the righteous one" (see Acts 3:14; 7:52; 22:14).

Paul takes this understanding of righteousness and fills it out with the person of Jesus Christ. He sees that in Christ there is a new way of conceiving of God's covenant people. The problem is laid out dramatically in the first two chapters of Romans.

All have broken the obligations of the covenant community. It was expected that Gentiles would have failed in this regard, because they had always stood outside the covenant community. But Paul drives home the point that the Jews had failed as well. All deserve the just sentence of the righteous judge.

Instead, God has done something marvelous and righteous. He has in some sense changed the terms of the covenant, or better, helped us grasp its deeper dimension: "But now the righteousness of God has been manifested apart from the law, although the Law and the Prophets bear witness to it—the righteousness of God through faith in Jesus Christ for all who believe" (Rom. 3:21–22).

The terms of the covenant require a righteous God to act according to those terms, and the consequences of breaking the covenant, as put in Isaiah are "you shall be eaten by the sword" (1:20)—that is, the ultimate consequence is death.

But Paul says there is a righteous one who stood in the place of all who have disobeyed. He suffered the death that was due the covenant breakers. He endured the just consequences of the broken covenant: to be forsaken by God.

And thus God remains the righteous judge: "This was to show God's righteousness, because in his divine forbearance he had passed over former sins. It was to show his righteousness at the present time, so that he might be just and the justifier of the one who has faith in Jesus" (Rom. 3:25–26).

Where does that leave the covenant people and the non-covenant people (the Gentiles)? It invites them all to participate in the new covenant community, one whose initiation rite is to trust in Jesus Christ, the righteous one. Thus all who believe in this gospel, this message of Good News, are "in Christ" and thus part of the covenant community.

When the New Testament writers say that believers have righteousness, then, they primarily mean they have "covenant membership," that is, right standing in the kingdom community. Only secondarily does righteousness refer to the type of behavior those in this community strive to live by. It is only in this context that we can understand properly the call to "pursue righteousness, godliness, faith, love, steadfastness, gentleness" (1 Tim. 6:11).

Now, finally, we can come back to address our original concerns.

The righteous God is not, as we are wont to think, primarily one who is morally upright to an infinite degree. This indeed would be a God we would end up either hating or at least being indifferent toward.

Instead, the righteous God is one who creates community. In the light of Christ, that community is now a community of faith. As we view the biblical narrative we see that this God will do whatever is necessary—including dying for his people—to ensure that they remain connected to that community.

Similarly, God wants to bestow righteousness upon us. But that doesn't mean primarily that he wants to make us paragons of virtue—new Pharisees or Puritans. He's not placing on our backs new burdens to fulfill a myriad of religious obligations. No! When God calls us "righteous," he means to say that we are now part of his kingdom community.

To be sure, there are covenantal obligations to fulfill; that is, a certain moral course to follow in life. But it is not as if perfect fulfillment of those obligations is the key to membership in this community or the ultimate definition of righteousness. No, we are righteous because we first are members of the community of God.

Thus righteousness is grounded and fulfilled not in morally pure behavior but in relationship. Not primarily in adherence to some abstract set of laws but in the midst of community—the divine community we call the Trinity, and the earthly community we call the church. We were created for such community, for relationships, for love. And righteousness is one word that crystallizes all that.

That's why we often find the biblical writers praising God's righteousness and why metaphors of the most personal kind are used when they write about it:

> Let me hear what God the LORD will speak,
>   for he will speak peace to his people, to his saints;
>   but let them not turn back to folly.
> Surely his salvation is near to those who fear him,
>   that glory may dwell in our land.
> Steadfast love and faithfulness meet;
>   righteousness and peace kiss each other.
>
> Psalm 85:8–10

Righteousness here embraces terms we are immediately attracted to, like *steadfast love*, *faithfulness*, and *peace*. Righteousness does not tear us apart but enables us to embrace each other and our God. It's not about the shaking of the finger but about kissing with the lips.

So if you like kissing, you'll like righteousness.

10

Beyond Manipulation (Merciful)

God, be merciful to me, a sinner!

Luke 18:13

Most of the attributes discussed in this book point to God's transcendence. In this age of intimacy, transcendence tends to put us off. Thus my attempt to show how transcendence is ultimately the ground of God's nearness to us.

We might think that with *mercy*, finally, we've come to an attribute that we can easily warm up to. I don't know. Mercy may be the most difficult attribute to accept.

The act of mercy, at its biblical core, is an act of pure grace, that is, unmerited favor. It is a favor extended to a person in need. Neither of these propositions—that we do not merit favor, that we are in need—sit well with us. They remind us of pity, and who today wants to be pitied? So we spend most of our lives fighting mercy, and only in the face of death do we finally grasp our pitiful situation for what it is, and embrace mercy with all our hearts, souls, minds, and strength.

We are well aware that there is "a problem with the human condition." We see evil unleashed like a tsunami, causing all sorts of destruction everywhere on the planet. We in the church have been trained to say we are sinners in need of grace, so it trips off the tongue easily. At some moments we actually believe it.

But many days we're like the rich young ruler. When Jesus told him to obey the Ten Commandments, he replied, "Teacher, all these I have kept from my youth" (Mark 10:20).

I'll be honest: some nights I go to bed trying to think of sins to confess for the day, and I just can't bring anything significant to mind. A peccadillo here, a minor infraction there—I took an extra fifteen minutes for lunch break, I interrupted my wife at dinner, and so forth. To be frank, I was so busy doing the work God has called me to do—managing a team of editors to produce a magazine—that I hardly had time to covet my neighbor's wife or to bear false witness. And since my parents are deceased and it wasn't the Sabbath, I could hardly break those commandments.

I might as well say, "Lord, I've pretty much kept the commandments today." Surely Jesus didn't have to die on the cross because I took an extra fifteen minutes for lunch.

Closely related is our inability to believe in the consequences of sin. That also comes with the spirit of the age, an age that does not really believe in consequences.

This is the logic of credit card debt. The idea is to buy now and pay later. But a lot of people never get around to paying, because paying seems like such a pain. When push comes to shove, we refinance, and then refinance again, and eventually declare bankruptcy, wait a few years, and start all over again.

I, like many people, have more credit card debt than I feel comfortable with, and so I know the temptation whereof I speak. It is the temptation to deny consequences.

The same sort of thinking underlies the lack of retirement savings in the United States. Most of us simply have not saved enough to tide us over through our retirement years. The notion is not spend now and pay later but spend now and save later. You'd think that this logic would catch up with spenders after a while and that the fear of poverty in old age would instill the discipline of saving. But the baby boomer generation, of which I am a member, has shown that human nature can blissfully ignore future consequences. None of us believes that Social Security will survive, but we're all hoping against hope that it does. Somebody, somewhere will figure out the solution. In the meantime, we're on the Internet surfing for deals on plasma TVs.

One of Jesus's parables, found in Luke 16:19–31, speaks indirectly about this problem. In it he describes two men. The first is a wealthy man, always impeccably dressed and sumptuously fed; the second is a diseased and impoverished man named Lazarus, who would have been happy eating the scraps from the rich man's table. They both die. Lazarus ends up in heaven, the rich man in Hades, and between them lies a great chasm that cannot be bridged.

The rich man, heedless of the consequences during his life, has at least the wherewithal to try to warn his loved ones. He calls out to father Abraham in heaven, pleading with him to send Lazarus back to earth: "I beg you, father, to send him to my father's house—for I have five brothers—so that he may warn them, lest they also come into this place of torment" (vv. 27–28).

Abraham knows they don't need a miracle, they just need the good sense to read and obey the wisdom they've heard time and again: "They have Moses and the Prophets," he replies, "let them hear them" (v. 29).

The rich man insists: "No, father Abraham, but if someone goes to them from the dead, they will repent" (v. 30).

But father Abraham knows human nature: "If they do not hear Moses and the Prophets," he says, "neither will they be convinced if someone should rise from the dead" (v. 31).

"The wages of sin is death," says Paul (Rom. 6:23). The crucifixion is the death that substitutes for our death. The resurrection is an overcoming of death, indeed, but at the same time a sobering sign that the consequences of sin are so catastrophic that a miracle is required to overcome them. You'd think with all this death-talk in Scripture, we'd get the idea.

And yet it's a rare day when I can fathom how my sins deserve death. The peccadilloes deserve a slap on the wrist, for sure. Everyone needs a little accountability. But mercy? Do I really need to act like and be treated like (to use the famous phrase from the Book of Common Prayer) a "miserable sinner"?

Even my lust and greed and covetousness—all of which amounts to idolatry, according to Scripture—hardly strike me as worthy of death, that is, eternal separation from the presence of God. This would be like disowning your child for lying to you, or divorcing your spouse for burning dinner.

Come on. God couldn't care that much about sin, could he?

After all, we reason, it's God's job to forgive.

This certainly seems to be the theme of Scripture. Even when he's angry as hell and doesn't want to take it anymore, he's constantly overruling himself. God speaks through the prophet Hosea:

> When Israel was a child, I loved him,
>   and out of Egypt I called my son.
> The more they were called,
>   the more they went away;
> they kept sacrificing to the Baals
>   and burning offerings to idols.

Hosea 11:1–2

And then God goes on to describe the wrath he intends to execute:

> They shall not return to the land of Egypt,
>   but Assyria shall be their king,
>   because they have refused to return to me.
> The sword shall rage against their cities,
>   consume the bars of their gates,
>   and devour them because of their own counsels.
> My people are bent on turning away from me,
>   and though they call out to the Most High,
>   he shall not raise them up at all.

Hosea 11:5–7

This is an appropriate and just response. But then God suddenly backpedals:

> How can I give you up, O Ephraim?
>   How can I hand you over, O Israel?
> How can I make you like Admah?
>   How can I treat you like Zeboiim?
> My heart recoils within me;
>   my compassion grows warm and tender.
> I will not execute my burning anger;
>   I will not again destroy Ephraim;
> for I am God and not a man,
>   the Holy One in your midst,
>   and I will not come in wrath.

Hosea 11:8–9

No wonder we glibly think it is God's business to forgive. When push comes to shove, he doesn't have any judgmental backbone. It seems we do not have a need for mercy as much as God has a need to forgive.

We may not be horrible creatures deserving annihilation, and it may be God's business to forgive, but it remains our business to do what we can to deserve forgiveness. We're not thrilled about mercy, in the end, because we honestly feel it is within our power to merit absolution.

We're not as crass as the Pharisee, in the parable of the Pharisee and the tax collector. The Pharisee prayed, "God, I thank you that I am not like other men, extortioners, unjust, adulterers, or even like this tax collector. I fast twice a week; I give tithes of all that I get" (Luke 18:11–12). We're smart enough to see the pride that saturates this prayer.

And we recognize a lot of ourselves in the tax collector, who prays, "God, be merciful to me, a sinner!" (Luke 18:13).

But here's how we can subtly subvert even this prayer for mercy: we start imagining that *our penitent attitude* is the cause of God's being merciful to us. If we confess our sins *with meaning*, and *feel contrite* in our hearts, God will surely forgive. Thus confession and contrition become the works that open the doors to heaven.

In essence, we don't feel we need mercy as much as we need to show God how sorry we are. Then all will be well.

All of these rationalizations stem from our deep discomfort with appearing needy and undeserving.

My neighbor has a snowblower, which he apparently loves to use. So two or three times a winter, he blows clean not only the sidewalks around my house but also my driveway. As much as I appreciate it, it makes me feel uncomfortable.

One summer day, as I finished edging my lawn with my power edger, I noticed his lawn's ragged edges. *Aha! I can pay him back!* I thought. So now I edge his lawn regularly.

It would be unthinkable to leave the ledger unbalanced, as if I were in debt and therefore needy and he were not. To be sure, I also don't want to appear ungrateful, so naturally I look for ways to thank him. But I have to admit that this need to appear un-needy drives much of this quid pro quo ("something for something").

Nearly everything in our culture is, in fact, driven by the quid pro quo. As children mature, they absorb this reigning cultural value, so they are anxious to get out from under the umbrella of paternalism into a life of independence. And for the same reason, the elderly do not go off gently into the night but fight vigorously to retain their independence, to live at home and to drive. Nobody wants to be dependent on others.

While there is a measure of maturity in this attitude— indeed, we should all be contributing members of society— this quid pro quo instinct has no place when it comes to our relationship with God. This is one reason the life of faith is so difficult, why it takes a lifetime to learn how to walk this peculiar walk, why it's usually not until we face death that we get it.

The reality is, however, that we have absolutely nothing to offer God that he needs or wants. He did not create us to fill a void in his life. He created us out of the sheer pleasure of creating. He does not need us to love him, because he knows perfect love in his own being as Father, Son, and Holy Spirit. He does not need us to accomplish his will in the world. He's omnipotently capable of doing that by himself, thank you very much.

Add to this how utterly disappointing we are to God, and we will stand at the threshold of mercy. It's not the peccadilloes that concern God. He sees them for what they are better than we do. It's the overall direction of our being that troubles him. As the song says, we're always looking for love in all the wrong places. Like that passage in Hosea put it:

> The more they were called,
>   the more they went away;
>   they kept sacrificing to the Baals
>   and burning offerings to idols.

Hosea 11:2

We have before us the almighty and all-loving God, in whose image we've been created, in whose being we are sustained moment by moment, in whose love we are invited to bask—and we give ourselves to every dime-store god (mainly money, sex, and power) that comes along promising us a new thrill.

Day by day we live in a rather startling state of denial. As noted above, we just refuse to face the reality of our situation. It's not easy to do, because to face it means to confront nasty and horrific facts about ourselves and about our destiny outside of God. There's a reason that the words *sin* and *judgment* and *hell* have been driven from our vocabulary. They just bring up all sorts of thoughts we'd just as soon not have to deal with.

We really are pitiful creatures. If anyone treated us like we treat our Creator, if anyone lived in such an obtuse state of denial about something so catastrophic—well, we'd dismiss them as both ungrateful and hopeless.

To seek to be in relationship with a merciful God means to abandon all claims on him. In some sense, it means to abandon all assumptions about him, like the assumption that if we do X he will do Y.

To seek God's mercy means, paradoxically, abandoning any right to mercy and any hope of mercy. To know that we are utterly needy and utterly dependent means to go to God

110

with the frightening realization that he would be perfectly just and right to simply ignore our prayer. This is part of what it means to fear the Lord and why fear is the beginning of wisdom. Fear in the presence of God is, finally, an honest realization of where we stand in the cosmos—condemned and unworthy—if he were anything else but the God he is.

It means we recognize that it is not that our confession and contrition moves God but that God has first prompted us to confession and contrition. We could never feel contrition unless the Spirit had already been working mercifully within us. The act of contrition is, in one sense, both a confession and a thanksgiving for the gift of contrition.

There is a way to say, "God, be merciful to me, a sinner," that looks for a quid pro quo. And there is a way to say it as a humble acknowledgment of how dependent we are on God's gracious favor.

That is the nature of the perfect humility that seeks mercy.

But here's the rub: we can rarely if ever approach God with perfect humility. We're always looking for something from God, always looking to finagle something out of him. We may confess our sins because we finally recognize our shortcomings, but we're also anxious to rid ourselves of these nasty feelings of guilt. And if God is the one who can do that, we'll go to God.

So I find that even in my most humble moments, I'm still trying to manipulate God to make myself feel better. This is not a humility that seeks mercy but a scheming that's trying to get something out of God.

But God is so merciful that he sees our schemes for what they are. He sees the narcissism that wraps its tentacles even around our abject prayer, "God, be merciful to me, a sinner." He knows that even our humility is stained with pride and that our acknowledgment of need is mixed with a longing for a quid pro quo.

More frightening still, God knows with how much contempt we've treated his mercy. John Bunyan, author of *Pilgrim's Progress*, said sin "is the dare of his justice, the rape of his mercy, the jeer of his patience, the slight of his power, and the contempt of his love."[1] It's not just that our motives, even at their best, are mixed. It's that in the end, we have no idea how holy mercy is and how often we profane it.

God is such that he looks at our ridiculousness, our convoluted piety and confused contrition, our blasphemy of mercy—and he just gives up. "This people just don't get it," he says. "They never will. They're hopeless."

Then he throws up his hands—and stretches out his arms, and embraces us in mercy. Pure, unadulterated mercy. We continue to squirm in his arms, like a child who thinks he's too grown up to be hugged, but if we've got any sense at all, we won't try to break free.

11

Fierce Passion
(Jealous)

For you shall worship no other god, for the LORD, whose name is Jealous, is a jealous God.

Exodus 34:14

I remember the first time I was jealous. It was a most unpleasant experience.

I was in college, and I had just started a relationship with the woman who was to become my wife. I was walking across a footbridge that separated the dorms from the center of campus. I looked to my right, and I could see Barbara through a dorm window. Seeing Barb was the sort of thing that gave me great delight. What didn't give me delight was that she was in a room with a mutual male friend. He was on the top bunk, lying face down, and she was standing next to him with her hand on his shoulder.

The proverbial stab went through my heart. Not the stab of love, but of jealousy. Barbara and I had made no promises to one another. We weren't "going steady," as we said back then. But it was clear that we had a deepening relationship. When I saw her in what appeared to be a very personal conversation with another man, I was filled with a mixture of envy and anger.

I tried to keep walking, but jealousy stopped me in my tracks. I kept peering into the window, looking for signs that would help me discern exactly what was going on. When I finally did move on, I couldn't get the scene out of my mind. I started rehearsing all sorts of ways to ask her casually what was going on with her and Mike, without of course sounding like I was jealous.

I've only experienced this emotion a couple of times since, and it was equally disturbing. Each time I could see that it was rooted in a combination of vices I thought I had mastered: distrust, suspicion, controlling behavior, anger, and possessiveness.

Therapists tell us how jealousy undermines a relationship; preachers warn how it sabotages the soul. One biblical proverb implies that it is one of the most destructive of traits: "Wrath is cruel, anger is overwhelming, but who can stand before jealousy?" (Prov. 27:4).

So it is not a little puzzling that God is associated with jealousy over thirty times in the Bible and, worse, that he claims it as essential to his identity: "For you shall worship no other god, for the LORD, whose name is Jealous, is a jealous God" (Exod. 34:14).

We could dismiss this as a momentary metaphor lapse by biblical writers and fashion a historical-critical reason to ignore it. But not only is God's jealousy mentioned over thirty times, the mentions come at the most crucial moments in Israel's history, such as the giving of the Ten Commandments:

> You shall have no other gods before me. You shall not make for yourself a carved image, or any likeness of anything that

114

is in heaven above, or that is in the earth beneath, or that is in the water under the earth. You shall not bow down to them or serve them, for I the LORD your God am a jealous God.

Exodus 20:3–5

No, this cannot be passed off as a culturally relative notion, nor a copyist's error. God, it seems, wishes to be known as a jealous God.

Jealousy, of course, is associated with love—"Jealousy and love are sisters" is the way a Russian proverb puts it. Saint Augustine noted this relationship when he said, "He that is not jealous is not in love." Or to put it the other way, only one who loves can know jealousy. I would not have been jealous of Barbara had she been merely a friend. Because I was falling in love with her, suddenly jealousy became a possibility.

My jealousy, as I said, contained a strong dose of possessiveness: I was jealous because I did not want to share Barbara's love with anyone else. It had a measure of rivalry: I didn't want another man to take Barbara from me. It included a pinch of anger: I felt betrayed by Barbara. And so on.

In human beings, these are vices. They arise out of an inflated sense of the self, the assumption that what I want for the other person is best for the other person. Barbara's love should focus exclusively on me. Jealousy is the desire to be god to another.

While it is inappropriate for humans to assume God's prerogatives, it is praiseworthy for God to do so. Human beings have no right to possess another human life—that's called involuntary servitude. God, our creator and redeemer, has every right to possess us. This is why the devout of all eras have been happy to call themselves "servants" or even "slaves" of God.

Human beings have no right to demand the ultimate loyalty of another human being. We are flawed, finite, selfish beings. God, on the other hand, is holy, infinite, and perfectly loving. He deserves everyone's ultimate loyalty.

In a paradoxical way, when we experience jealousy, we experience something of the life of God. The difference is that we do not have the prerogative to be jealous. He does.

When God sees his people traipsing after other gods, he would hardly be a God of love if he remained indifferent. The other gods are false. They are destructive to human flowering. Today's false gods—pleasure, success, entertainment, wealth, and so forth—bring momentary happiness but fragment the soul. A soul that is broken over and over may, at some point, be impossible to put back together again.

God loves his people, and the last thing he wants to see them do is skip down a path that leads to their own destruction. You bet he's jealous.

We see this noble jealousy in parents often. In Marilynne Robinson's novel *Gilead*, the narrator, the Rev. John Ames, is coming to the end of his life, and he writes a letter to his son. One thing that concerns Ames is the relationship that another man is striking up with his son. He knows a great deal about this man and knows he is a man of questionable character. So he wants to warn his son about the dangers of this man becoming the boy's father figure when Ames passes on:

> My impulse is strong to warn you against Jack Boughton. Your mother and you. You may know what a fallible man I am, and how little I can trust my feelings on the subject. And you know, from living out years I cannot foresee, whether you must forgive me for warning you, or forgive me for failing to warn you, or indeed if none of it turned out to matter at all. . . . He is not a man of the highest character. Be wary of him.[1]

Ames is conflicted about whether he should do this. He questions his motives. But as the novel unfolds, we see that his warning arises out of a holy jealousy. He loves his son dearly, and he does not want to see his son get hurt or be influenced by this man of less than "the highest character."

Such are the warnings of God to the people of Israel. The biblical writers harped on God's jealousy because they wanted to communicate that God was the guardian of Israel. Who wouldn't want a divine protector to guard them like a jealous lover? In this respect, the biblical emphasis on God's jealousy tells us as much about the people as it does about God—their longing and gratefulness for a loving protector.

Since jealousy is tethered to love, the attribute also assumes a certain passion. I did not have a calm, rational desire to protect Barbara from what I (narcissistically) believed might be a bad influence on her. I was in love with Barbara and therefore passionate about this seemingly "dangerous" situation.

God's jealousy is not just a sign of protecting love but also of passionate engagement:

> Take care, lest you forget the covenant of the LORD your God, which he made with you, and make a carved image, the form of anything that the LORD your God has forbidden you. For the LORD your God is a consuming fire, a jealous God.
>
> Deuteronomy 4:23–24

A relationship with God is not a mechanical exercise, not a bureaucratic bestowing of welfare benefits by a disinterested but benevolent all-powerful being. On God's side, the biblical witness attests, are frustration, disappointment, anger, mourning, rage, compassion—the consuming fire of love.

All of these reactions come into play precisely because God has granted us a tremendous amount of freedom. He may not control our response to him, but that doesn't mean he is indifferent. He cares deeply, passionately. Frankly, he overdoes it! But such is the nature of perfect love. It is not a measured, rational love but one desperate for the welfare of the beloved. He will not, cannot, sit by and do nothing, say nothing, when his beloved acts foolishly—like following false gods, gods whose fruit can only be death.

That's why those who follow God most closely and love him most dearly end up acting like their Jealous Lover. Take Francis of Assisi.

Among his many virtues, Francis is known for his passionate embrace of poverty. Not only did he forbid his emerging Order to own property, he added this discipline for each of the brothers: "Let none of the brothers . . . wherever he may be or go, carry, receive, or have received in any way coin or money, whether for clothing, books, or payment for work."[2]

There were few exceptions. If a brother was sick or if someone needed medical attention, the brothers could beg for money to pay for a doctor or medicine. But other than that, they were to never touch money. In fact, they were forbidden from even being seen with a beggar who asked for money.

Francis was passionate about this rule, jealous for obedience to it: "If by chance, God forbid, it happens that some brother is collecting or holding coin or money," he wrote in his earlier rule, "let all the brothers consider him a deceptive brother, an apostate, a thief, a robber."[3]

It was a passion without patience. According to an early collection of Francis stories, a layman entered the headquarters of the Order, Saint Mary of the Portiuncula, to pray. He also left an offering, laying some coins near the cross. Later that day, a brother saw the coins and unthinkingly picked them up and placed them on a window ledge.

Later, the brother realized what he had done. He also heard that Francis had found out. He was horrified, so he immediately rushed to Francis and implored forgiveness. He told Francis to whip him for penance.

Francis was not so easily placated. Instead, after rebuking the brother, he told him to go to the windowsill, pick up a coin with his mouth, and carry it outside. Then, with the coin still in his mouth, he was to deposit it in a heap of ass's dung. The brother obeyed gladly.[4]

This is extreme discipleship, to say the least. But Francis knew that money was like a drug, as addictive and destructive to the soul as cocaine is to the body. Francis did not believe money could be used moderately or "recreationally" without it eventually enslaving. He believed Jesus literally: one cannot serve God and mammon (see Matt. 6:24).

In short, he was so jealous for God, so passionate about a fully realized relationship with him, that he acted in ways we consider "over the top." But this is the sort of thing love does to a person. Passionate jealousy walks hand in hand with love.

At the end of the Earlier Rule, Francis appended a poetic exhortation that reveals the extent of his desire for God:

> Therefore,
> let us desire nothing else,
> let us want nothing else,
> let nothing else please us and cause us delight except
>   our Creator, Redeemer, and Savior,
> the only true God,
> Who is the fullness of good,
> All good, every good, the true and supreme good,
> Who alone is good,
> Merciful, gentle, delightful, and sweet,
> Who alone is holy,
> Just, true, holy, and upright,
> Who alone is kind, innocent, clean,
> From whom, through whom, and in whom
> Is all pardon, all grace, all glory
> Of all penitents and just ones,
> Of all the blessed rejoicing together in heaven.[5]

This passion led Francis to say and do the most extravagant things. And he learned this from the God named Jealous, the consuming fire, who wants nothing but the absolute best for us. He's given us freedom to choose our way, but he's not going to let it go at that. He is not ashamed to stoop to any behavior, even fits of jealous rage, to get our attention so that we might reject lesser loves.

Such a God is not an easy deity to deal with all the time. But I would not want to have any other God on my side.

12

Redeeming Anger
(Wrath)

> He will tread the winepress of the fury of the wrath
> of God the Almighty.
>
> Revelation 19:15

One cannot talk about the jealousy of God without also talking about the wrath of God. Nearly every verse that speaks of God's jealousy also speaks of his anger. One example among many:

> You shall not go after other gods, the gods of the peoples who are around you, for the LORD your God in your midst is a jealous God—lest the anger of the LORD your God be kindled against you, and he destroy you from off the face of the earth.
>
> Deuteronomy 6:14–15

If jealousy is a troublesome attribute to ponder, God's anger is more so. A God of wrath appears to us as a vengeful, violent

121

deity, one who seems just as likely to destroy as he is to save. That appears utterly incompatible with the God of love. This is not a God we're much interested in meeting.

But we keep bumping into him in the Bible. This would be an easy God to sidestep if the Bible was just another book. But the church has for some time taught that this book is nothing less than the revelation of God to man.

Some have argued that perhaps this angry deity is the God of the Old Testament, but the God of the New Testament—who comes to us in Jesus Christ—is a God of love. That would be a persuasive argument except for two things.

First, we have plenty of moments in the Old Testament where God's compassion and mercy overflow the pages.

> The LORD is merciful and gracious,
>   slow to anger and abounding in steadfast love.
> He will not always chide,
>   nor will he keep his anger forever.
> He does not deal with us according to our sins,
>   nor repay us according to our iniquities.
> For as high as the heavens are above the earth,
>   so great is his steadfast love toward those who fear
>   him;
> as far as the east is from the west,
>   so far does he remove our transgressions from us.
> As a father shows compassion to his children,
>   so the LORD shows compassion to those who fear
>   him.
> For he knows our frame;
>   he remembers that we are dust.
>
> Psalm 103:8–14

Second, we have plenty of moments in the New Testament where God incarnate seems as angry as the stereotyped Old Testament God. Take these examples just from the Gospel of Mark:

122

- Jesus "sternly charges" or "strictly orders" (depending on the translation) people he heals (1:43; 3:12; 5:43; 8:30). He looks upon religious leaders with "anger" and "grief" (3:5).

- He speaks of a sin which God will never forgive (3:29), of horrific consequences for misleading children (9:42), of God being ashamed with some at the Judgment (8:38).

- Jesus destroys a herd of swine without regret or compensation to the owner (5:1–20) and overturns the tables in the temple in a moment of rage (11:15–17).

- He rebukes Peter as demonic (8:33); he is "indignant" with the disciples (10:13–14); the Sadducees, he says, are biblically and spiritually ignorant (12:24); and his entire generation he describes as "faithless" (9:19).

- He makes it clear that following him will entail suffering and death (9:35–37; 8:35–37). The end times judgment, which he says will come sooner than anyone thinks, will be so severe that even the faithful will beg for death (13:5–37).

This tension I address at book length in *Jesus Mean and Wild: The Unexpected Love of an Untamable God*; I try to show the many ways in which anger and love are not opposites but kissing cousins. One example will have to suffice here.

A child chases a ball into the street, into the path of a speeding car. At the last second, the car swerves and brakes and misses the child by inches. The mother comes running out, picks the child up firmly, and plants him on the sidewalk—and proceeds to give him the lecture of his young life. "What were you thinking? How many times have I told you not to step into the street without looking? If this is how you behave when I'm not looking. . . ." And so on.

There is no empathetic understanding: "I can imagine how excited you were playing catch, and of course you lost track.

It happens to all of us." No patient pedagogy: "Now next time the ball ends up in the street, here's what you can do. . . ."

Instead, the child received a verbal lashing he will not soon forget. The mother may not even feel she has done her job unless she can bring the child to tears. She is desperate that he comprehend the danger, that he obey her, that he never, ever forget. Is she cruel or abusive or arbitrary? Hardly. She is a mother who so loves her son that she is willing to shock him to save his life.

Much of God's wrath can be understood as the response of a God who passionately loves and will do anything, including shake up his beloved, if he thinks it will help them pay attention to things that need attention.

Since I finished *Jesus Mean and Wild*, I've been reminded that despite the apparent offensiveness of God's anger, a part of us instinctively longs for the wrath of God—particularly at the last judgment.

The author of the book of Revelation traffics in dramatic imagery and metaphors, but not without reason. He was writing to a beleaguered church that needed to understand that the ultimate victory in history belongs not to the enemies of God but to Jesus Christ and his followers. In Revelation, Jesus Christ is depicted as the one who executes God's fierce wrath:

> Then I saw heaven opened, and behold, a white horse! The one sitting on it is called Faithful and True, and in righteousness he judges and makes war. His eyes are like a flame of fire, and on his head are many diadems, and he has a name written that no one knows but himself. He is clothed in a robe dipped in blood, and the name by which he is called is The Word of God. And the armies of heaven, arrayed in fine linen, white and pure, were following him on white horses. From his mouth comes a sharp sword with which to strike down the nations, and he will rule them with a rod of iron. *He*

will tread the winepress of the fury of the wrath of God the Almighty.
On his robe and on his thigh he has a name written, King of
kings and Lord of lords.

Revelation 19:11–16, emphasis added

From there it gets gruesome, with birds that "eat the flesh
of kings, the flesh of captains, the flesh of mighty men" (Rev.
19:18). The great enemies of God, the beast and the false
prophet and all who followed them, are "thrown alive into the
lake of fire that burns with sulfur. And the rest were slain by
the sword that came from the mouth of him who was sitting
on the horse, and all the birds were gorged with their flesh"
(Rev. 19:20–21).

This is not a happy scene; it is R-rated, to be sure. In the
end, all those who have warred against God and his people,
who remain unrepentant and hateful toward the things of
God, will endure the wrath of God.

The wrath in this biblical picture, of course, is still an expression of love, but love for the people of God. For they are
the ones who have endured mockery, persecution, and slaying
at the hands of "the beast" and the "false prophet" and those
who followed him. In other words, wrath is an extension of
the justice of God.

This is a wrath we can sympathize with. This is the wrath
Americans felt after 9/11 and Pearl Harbor, and the wrath
Northerners felt during the Civil War. In the latter case, for
example, they felt a palpable sense that the evils of slavery
needed to end and that war was part of the divine retribution
for this social sin. Julia Ward Howe captured this sense when
she penned her famous hymn, which begins,

> Mine eyes have seen the glory of the coming of the
> Lord:
> He is trampling out the vintage where the grapes of
> wrath are stored;

He hath loosed the fateful lightning of His terrible
swift sword:
His truth is marching on.[1]

Abraham Lincoln nuanced this sense of divine wrath in
his second inaugural address, recognizing that it was in some
sense visited on both North and South for the sins of the
entire nation:

Fondly do we hope, fervently do we pray, that this mighty
scourge of war may speedily pass away. Yet, if God wills that
it continue until all the wealth piled by the bondsman's two
hundred and fifty years of unrequited toil shall be sunk, and
until every drop of blood drawn with the lash shall be paid
by another drawn with the sword, as was said three thousand
years ago, so still it must be said "the judgments of the Lord
are true and righteous altogether."[2]

While justice meted out in history usually has this am-
biguous cast—the guilty and innocent must sometimes both
suffer for the sins of the nation—at the end of history,
no such ambiguity will be known. The stubborn and vicious enemies of justice and love—enemies of God—will
be judged.

In the end, God's severe wrath is not directed against the
ignorant, nor against the indifferent or the lost; he still tries to
woo, even coerce, these into his family. But against the knowing, active, and unrepentant enemies of justice and love, he
only displays wrath—the wrath of a mother bear protecting
her cubs from a threat. It is reserved for unrepentant racists,
for hardened purveyors of genocide, for callous abusers of
women and children, for those who shed deliberately the
blood of the innocent—for those who have indeed become
the enemies of God and of man.

If this God remains offensive to modern moral sensibilities, we must instead question those sensibilities. If this God
disturbs us, it may be because we have lost our capacity to

be horrified by injustice. If God is supposed to give a pass to these tyrants of history, then he is no longer a God of the just, and we should have nothing to do with him.

While God's wrath remains even in Jesus Christ, God's attitude toward his creation still makes a noticeable shift in the light of Jesus Christ. No question that we're dealing with the same God, a God who displays loving anger and angry love sometimes. But something has fundamentally changed.

In the Old Testament, people knew of God's anger and experienced it as such. It led to both types of fear. Fear plain and simple—that sense that God was one who could very well destroy in an instant. But also fear in the sense of awe and respect.

But the fear of God as one who can instantly annihilate is no longer possible in the light of Jesus Christ. There may have been a time when it was unclear whether God's wrath would be executed finally, sweepingly against sinners. But because of the final and sweeping death of Jesus Christ, that fear is now unfounded. The battle of wrath and mercy for God's heart—at least the way the biblical writers dramatize it, especially Hosea—has been won by mercy.

But not at the expense of wrath. For wrath, as we recall, is nothing but anger at the stubborn evil of men and women, at the destructiveness of false religion, at the lost promise of divine love and blessing. But now the object of wrath is not his beloved but his only begotten. Some have called this "divine child abuse," but in doing so they have overlooked a great and marvelous mystery.

This divine wrath is not vented by the Father against the Son as much as inflicted by God on himself. It's as if he had done penance for our behavior, vicarious penance for his own creation. In the book of Genesis, God regrets what he has made and so destroys it, save Noah. In the

New Testament, God regrets what he has made, and he destroys himself.

I write with hyperbole to draw attention to the dramatic shift that has occurred in Jesus Christ. The wrath of God in the Old Testament is mostly a sign of God's displeasure with us. In the New Testament it is mostly a sign of the extent of his love for us, for he is willing, paradoxically, to endure the holy wrath we deserve.

Novelist and essayist Dorothy Sayers noted in a famous essay that it was not just a representative of man who hung on the cross but God himself—and that makes all the difference in how we understand this crucial moment in history:

> For what it means is this, among other things: that, for whatever reason, God chose to make man as he is—limited and suffering and subject to sorrows and death—he [God] had the honesty and the courage to take his own medicine. Whatever game he is playing with his creation, he has kept his own rules and played fair. He can exact nothing from man that he has not exacted from himself. He has himself gone through the whole of human experience, from the trivial irritations of family life and the cramping restrictions of hard work and lack of money to the worst horrors of pain and humiliation, defeat, despair, and death. When he was a man, he played the man. He was born in poverty and died in disgrace, and thought it was worthwhile.[3]

What it means is that God is the subject and object of his wrath. Those who avoid the path of wanton, vicious, and recalcitrant evil no longer need fear a wrath that threatens our existence. A disciplining anger, yes. Toughening love, yes. But a wrath before which we cower in abject fear, a wrath whose fire goes unquenched? Never.

PART 3

Attributes
of Love

13

Life That Bubbles Over (Trinity)

> The glory that you have given me I have given to them, that they may be one even as we are one, I in them and you in me, that they may become perfectly one.
>
> John 17:22–23

The opening liturgical prayer we use at my church goes like this:

Almighty God, to you all hearts are open, all desires known, and from you no secrets are hid: Cleanse the thoughts of our hearts by the inspiration of your Holy Spirit, that we may perfectly love you, and worthily magnify your holy Name; through Christ our Lord. Amen.

The prayer is set in a trinitarian frame: it is addressed to God, invoking the Holy Spirit, petitioning through Christ.

131

And the point? That we might "perfectly love" this trinitarian God.

To be awed by the theological profundity of the trinitarian God, yes. To be amazed by the symmetry of the divine being, certainly. But to be moved to *love*—well, that is not the first word that comes to mind when one thinks of the Holy Trinity.

When we break up the Trinity, we can do better. We can love "the Father" or "the Son" because we can conjure up images of a loving parent or of a compassionate Jesus reaching out to the lost and alone. Loving "the Spirit" is more of a challenge because it's hard to get your arms around *spirit*. But that challenge pales in comparison with loving "the Trinity"—an abstract, intellectual concept.

One can, of course, admire a beautiful concept, especially when it expresses real-life relationships. $E = MC^2$. Or $A^2 + B^2 = C^2$. And so on. The Trinity has this sort of abstract beauty, a beauty suggested in the Nicene Creed.

The Nicene Creed, recited weekly in many churches, is a product of early church debates over the exact nature of the Trinity, particularly the relation of the Father and the Son. It is also a product, by God's providence, of Neoplatonic philosophy, the intellectual environment of the day. This philosophy gave the church language by which we could fine-tune our understanding of God.

Thus the Nicene Creed uses *homoousios* (Greek, "of *the same* essence") to describe the relation of the Father and Son and not *homoiousios* (Greek, "of *similar* essence")—which was the view of the anti-trinitarians at the time. Jesus is described as "God from God, light from light, true God from true God . . . *of the same being* with the Father." Some lament the fact that a single Greek letter, an iota, led to deep divisions in the church, but in fact this iota makes all the difference in the world. Without it, as Athanasius argued in *On the Incarnation*, the church ends up with a mediator who is not capable of mediating God and man. He ends up being nothing more than another creature.

After more theological debates and wranglings, the church came up with a trinitarian formula that remains definitive, the Athanasian Creed (which, since it was composed about AD 500, could not have been written by Athanasius but certainly owes its substance to the great church father):

> Now this is the catholic faith: We worship one God in trinity and the Trinity in unity, neither confusing the Persons nor dividing the divine being.
>
> For the Father is one person, the Son is another, and the Spirit is still another.
>
> But the deity of the Father, Son, and Holy Spirit is one, equal in glory, coeternal in majesty. . . .
>
> The Father was neither made nor created nor begotten;
>
> the Son was neither made nor created, but was alone begotten of the Father;
>
> the Spirit was neither made nor created, but is proceeding from the Father and the Son.
>
> Thus there is one Father, not three fathers; one Son, not three sons; one Holy Spirit, not three spirits.[1]

A symbol of this overall approach to the Trinity was created in the Middle Ages and is called the Shield of the Trinity:[2]

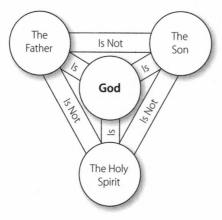

It is clear.

It is logical.

It is symmetrical.

A beauty to admire, but not quite something to love. Though theologians talk about the "persons" of the Trinity, the talk tends not to be very personal.

When Scripture talks about God, the language gets very personal.[3] Note how Jesus talked about his relationship to the Father in this prayer for his disciples:

> The glory that you have given me I have given to them, that they may be one even as we are one, I in them and you in me, that they may become perfectly one, so that the world may know that you sent me and loved them even as you loved me.... I made known to them your name, and I will continue to make it known, that the love with which you have loved me may be in them, and I in them.
>
> John 17:22–23, 26

This prayer comes at the climax of chapters 14 through 17 in John's Gospel; these are chapters where Jesus highlights his unity with the Father and the Spirit with statements such as these:

- "If you had known me, you would have known my Father also" (John 14:7).
- "Whoever has seen me has seen the Father" (John 14:9).
- "I am in the Father and the Father is in me" (John 14:11).
- "When the Spirit of truth comes . . . he will not speak on his own authority, but whatever he hears he will speak, and he will declare to you the things that are to come. He will glorify me, for he will take what is mine and declare it to you" (John 16:13–14).

This is a unity that transcends a formal and logical unity. It is a unity of purpose, as Jesus notes. But it is more: it is a unity of love.

And more still: most biblical passages about God's love emphasize God's love toward us. This only makes sense, since the main purpose of the Bible is not about the ontological nature of God but to tell of God's love affair with us. Yet in John 17 we are given a glimpse, if a brief one, into the life of the Trinity, into the dynamics of God as he is in himself. What Jesus clearly reveals is that God's love exists apart from his love from us—"I am in the Father and the Father is in me" (John 14:11).

So much of our love is based on our need for love. We enter into many relationships—friendships and marriage, in particular—not because we want to love and expect nothing in return. No, we say we want to share love with others. We want to love them, but we expect that in the normal course of the relationship, they will reciprocate with love. When this doesn't happen, the relationship falls apart.

This is true even as we try to reach out to the desperately needy. At one church, I struck up a relationship with a very needy woman. She could not get to church on her own, so I was one of the people who drove her to and from church regularly. She had problems with her parents, with friends, with memories, with self-confidence—and on it went. After spending many hours in conversation with her in the car and over the phone, I realized that in all the months we had been talking, she had not once asked me how I was, nor inquired about the welfare of my family. She didn't express any kind of concern for me, and I started to become resentful.

God is not like this. God's love for us is not based on his need for love nor on a need to be thanked. No, this God has known love, and perfect love at that, from before the creation of time and space. He created us not because he needed someone to return love to him but because the love of the Father, Son, and Holy Spirit bubbled over into creation.

God is slumming when he loves us. He doesn't *need* our mediocre love. He loves us because, well, he simply wants to. The "doctrine of the Trinity," it turns out, is not so much a logical and symmetrical way of thinking about God but more an entryway to love.

As such, it is also an entry into the very life of the Trinity.[4] Again in John, Jesus prays for his disciples—and us— asking "that they may all be one, just as you, Father, are in me, and I in you" (John 17:21). The three persons of the Trinity dwell in one another in an ongoing movement of love. Since we are made in the image of the Trinity, we are called to dwell in the life of the Trinity. Christ prays that we may share in the movement of love that passes between the divine persons, that we in some sense will be taken up into the Godhead.

This reality of a personal and organic union between God and man is not just a theme of John but is found in Paul— especially his repeated refrain about our being "in Christ"— and is expressed most succinctly by Peter, who says that by God's power, we may "become partakers of the divine nature" (2 Peter 1:4). This means not simply that we will grow to act like God acts—that is, become godly—but that we will partake of the love and fellowship of the Trinity.

This has all sorts of consequences, but one of particular import is this: when we partake of trinitarian love, our love begins to overflow as well. Jesus's two great commandments are not just obligations but descriptions of the spiritual life. It's not so much that we *have to* love God and then *have to* love our neighbor to be "good Christians." No, when we enter into the very fellowship of the Trinity, we enter a fellowship of love. What is that love like?

Well, we've noted how it so overflows, it creates other beings and enters into relations with those beings. On top of that, this love is driven to be in relationship with the creation, so that when the creation turned its face from its Creator, this love reached out to draw creation back to him. This love is willing to die to create fellowship once again.

As we enter into this fellowship of the Trinity, this very love is restored in us—and slowly, our love begins to overflow. Our love is now driven to seek out others. We look for ways to engage especially those who do not know love.

In the first epistle of John, we read that we cannot love God if we do not love our fellow man. This means not merely that the love of other is the sign of our love for God but that the two loves are inextricably linked. As Eastern Orthodox bishop Timothy Ware wrote,

> Man, made in the image of the Trinity, can only realize the divine likeness if he lives a common life such as the Blessed Trinity lives: as the three persons of the Godhead "dwell" in one another, so a man must "dwell" in his fellow men, living not for himself alone, but in and for others.[5]

When we ponder and pray to the God who is Trinity, we are opening ourselves not only to love of God but also to love of neighbor. This seemingly abstract doctrine, it turns out, is the path to community divine and human, to a love that knows no bounds and continues to bubble over.

My friend too quickly pours me a beer into too small a glass. It foams over and runs down the side of the glass, over my fingers, spilling onto the countertop and my lap. We laugh at his clumsiness, at the mess, but it is a mess that only adds to the moment.

Such is the paradoxical life of God the Trinity. The doctrine is clear, logical, and symmetrical—like the label on a fine bottle of beer. But once you open up to this God, you are immersed in a community of love that bubbles over into that wonderful mess called life.

14

A Bridge Over the Chasm of Despair (Suffering)

That I may know him and the power of his resurrection, and may share his sufferings, becoming like him in his death.

Philippians 3:10

It is a question made famous by writer Philip Yancey, but in one form or another, it has been asked for a long time by morally sensitive people: where is God when it hurts?

The question unnerves us because it presumes a great chasm exists in the universe, a Grand Canyon of despair. On the far side of the canyon stands God. On our side of the canyon stands our hurt. The canyon is so wide, God appears as a speck on the horizon. Our pain looms so large before us, we sometimes cannot even make out that distant divine speck. The canyon is so deep, we fear to approach the edge lest we trip and fall into the abyss. *Where is God when it hurts?* presumes this great canyon, this unbridgeable gulf, this chasm as deep and wide as the gap between eternity and time, between holiness and sin.

On this side of the chasm stands hurt—pain, grief, illness, injustice, despair. This is life on earth, the warp and woof of history, the daily news, the endless prayer chain requests.

On the Monday after Easter Sunday one year—Bright Monday, as it's called liturgically—we gathered for prayer at the *Christianity Today* office as we do every Monday. That Bright Monday, one colleague requested prayer for a friend, a college student whose sister and mother and father—the rest of his family—were killed in a car accident during Holy Week. Another colleague requested prayer for the parents of a son who had overdosed. It was as if Easter never happened.

Where is God when it hurts?

Sometimes that question, like these examples show, is very, very personal. Sometimes it's more philosophical, but it doesn't seem to hurt any less.

At the beginning of 2008, people in Kenya started killing each other. There was an election, but the party that lost believed (with good reason) that the supposed victors stuffed the ballot boxes. The ruling party had for years favored its own people (the Kikuyus) and had ignored the needs of other Kenyans (like the Luos). The stolen election was the last straw.

There were demonstrations, which erupted into killings, which led to revenge. Before long, half a million were homeless and over a thousand lay dead. In one incident early on, fifty people were locked in a church, and then the church was burned to the ground, while women and children tried to claw their way out.

Just say "Darfur" and one thinks "genocide." Across the world, women are sold into sexual slavery, and in our own land, young men step into schools and churches and start firing automatic weapons, and before you know it, the carpet is stained with the blood of the innocent. And we haven't even begun to tally the suffering from disease and so-called "acts of God."

The morally sensitive know that this philosophical question sometimes feels as personal as if we'd been raped or stabbed or abused or betrayed. So whether we're talking about suffering on the other side of the globe or on this side of our street, the question is the same: where is God when it hurts?

On the far side of this Grand Canyon of despair stands God—the side of healing, of wholeness, of tranquility, of peace. This is the life of God, is it not? This is what religion is supposed to deliver, is it not?

> Ask, and it will be given to you; seek, and you will find; knock, and it will be opened to you.
>
> Matthew 7:7

> God is our refuge and strength, a very present help in trouble.
>
> Psalm 46:1

> Comfort, comfort my people, says your God.
>
> Isaiah 40:1

That's what religion is for—an all-powerful God delivering spiritual goods and services like help from our troubles, peace in our turmoil, healing from our infirmities, happiness in the midst of strife. Your best life now.

But we stack that up against our personal pain and the suffering of the world, and we're left speechless, except for that one haunting question.

141

We seek desperately to bridge this chasm. We try to throw the bridge of the intellect across it. We look to the engineers of theology and philosophy—pastors, teachers. But after twenty centuries, the engineers of the faith have done nothing better than throw up fifty feet of rational support. We walk to the end of it, having gotten some answers, but soon enough we find ourselves at the end, staring once again across the Grand Canyon of despair.

So we try to hurdle across it by heroic faith. We look to verses like "you have not because you ask not" (see James 4:2) and "If you have faith, you can move mountains" (see Matt. 17:20), and we assume that it's our fault that God is over there and our pain is over here. We've got to have more faith. We've got to jump the gap.

So like a religious Evel Knievel, we mount our rocket-powered motorcycle of faith, donning a helmet of prayer and a shining white jumpsuit of salvation. We rev the engine and start hurtling down the long runway, hoping against hope to bring our pain to him so he can heal—only to find ourselves halfway across the canyon with no power left, and then begins the free fall.

The sane among us give up those sorts of efforts sooner or later when they realize that, of course, the deeper reality is that we can do nothing to bridge this humanly unbridgeable divide. No, Jesus Christ is the only one who can connect our hurt with his love.

Where is God when it hurts? Well, he shows up as a helpless, vulnerable baby.

He shows up as a common laborer, sharing the struggles of all those who make their living by the sweat of their brow.

He shows up as one who weeps with those who weep, like the time he broke down at the death of his friend Lazarus.

He shows up as the one who prays the night before his execution, praying not like some Greek god, some heroic mythical figure who defies fate with bravado, but as one who sweats blood and begs to be saved.

He shows up on a cross, as one who knows that there are times when suffering is so excruciating and so unjust that it feels like we're on the other side of the chasm from God.

We discover in Christ that this question—where is God when it hurts?—is not new at all, nor is it a question that God himself has never heard. It's as if he created the question himself. It's a question the Son of God asked of his heavenly Father, except he put it this way: "My God, my God, why have you forsaken me?" (Mark 15:34).

It turns out, then, that there is no chasm, because the chasm has been bridged. The God who is way over there and our hurt that is way over here have been joined at the cross.

Where is God when it hurts? At the center of the cross.

What does that mean practically?

It means, first, that God can be found in the midst of the pain. He is to be found, to be sure, in the comfort, the healing, the peace we know as answer to prayer. The gospel is not a Greek tragedy. God does indeed heal. I have experienced physical healing in my own life, as have millions of others.

God does comfort and give strength. I still find myself amazed that at the death of each of my parents, God gave me solace and courage to be able to conduct their funerals. Many have known even more extraordinary comfort in the midst of extraordinary tragedy.

God does indeed bring peace, to our souls and between warring peoples and nations. The apartheid era in South Africa was a time when unspeakable violence was perpetrated on so many innocent lives by both sides. And yet the number of people who found, in the midst of that evil, the capacity to forgive can be understood only as a divine visitation.

Beth Savage was shot at a Christmas party in 1992, and her body remains so full of shrapnel, she sets off alarms at airports.

Her father went into deep depression after the shooting and died soon afterwards. But Savage says, "All in all, what I must say through the trauma of it all, I honestly feel richer. . . . I think it's given me the ability to relate to other people."

Neville Clarence was left totally blind when a bomb exploded near him in 1983, a bomb that killed nineteen and wounded over two hundred people. At the amnesty hearings, he approached the leader of the operation and said, "I forgive you for what you have done. I came to the trial to share my feelings with you. I wanted you to know that I harbour no feelings of revenge."

Jeanne Fourie's daughter Lyndi was a victim in the Heidelberg Bombing of 1993. At the criminal trial, she tried to shake the hands of the three men who planted the bomb. At a later amnesty hearing, she said to them, "I forgive you because my High Command demonstrated to me how to do that by forgiving his killers."[1]

God does make himself known in these gracious ways, even in the face of disturbing evil.

But if we identify God simply with comfort and peace and the good feelings we seek, we're looking for a false god, a god who is nothing more than a projection of the self. It's only when that false god is in mind that we can ask, "Where is God when it hurts?" because the assumption of that question is that God is only to be associated with healing and peace, when the God of the Bible, the God who comes to us in Jesus Christ, is also made known in suffering, sickness, and death.

This is a great mystery, but it is one that the spiritually mature have embraced from the beginning. Like the apostle Paul, who said, "that I may know him and the power of his resurrection, and may share his sufferings, becoming like him in his death" (Phil. 3:10). He wants to know the resurrection, to be sure. He's no masochist, no stoic, no disciple of Greek tragedy. He knows there is a power and a hope that breaks into our suffering and heals and brings life.

But he also knows that the Triune God cannot be equated simply with good feelings and high moments. His desire is also to share in Christ's sufferings and become like him in his death because he knows we cannot know the God who comes to us in Jesus Christ, the God who endured the sufferings of human life and death on a cross, unless we too know suffering and death. Paul knows that God and his redemptive power are to be found right in the midst of suffering, right at the heart of pain.

That means two things.

When it comes to our own personal pain, it means we have the freedom to acknowledge it, not deny it. It means we have the courage to explore it, not hide from it. It means not fighting it but letting it take you where it will—which is eventually to the solid rock of Jesus Christ.

I have a good friend out East who has lived since childhood with psychological pain, with feelings of inadequacy, with anxieties about being deserted. He's spent his life creating a life that is safe, secure, clean, busy. He cannot sit still; he's always doing something, anything—manicuring his lawn, bowling, waxing his car, watching TV. He's afraid that if he stops and thinks, the memories will come rushing at him, the hurt will overwhelm him, and he'll drown.

One evening when he was vacationing at a beach resort with his wife, he went swimming in the surf by himself. He made his way out toward the larger waves to do some body surfing and soon realized that the current had caught him and was taking him out to sea. He started swimming desperately toward shore, but as these things go, the tide just kept pulling him out to sea. He kept frantically paddling, but things just got worse. Finally he reached the point of exhaustion, and he remembers saying, "I give up."

It was at that moment that a wave—this is a true story—a great wave came along and pushed him toward shore, and it dropped him back on dry land.

Instead of fighting what appears to be the deadly current of pain, a hurt we think is threatening to suck us out to sea and drown us, we can let the current of pain take us where it will, because eventually it will dump us on solid ground.

But what about the pain we feel for all those elsewhere who suffer tragically? Where is God when these people hurt? In the midst of their suffering.

"'Lord, when did we see you hungry and feed you, or thirsty and give you drink?'" the people ask Jesus in the famous parable. "'And when did we see you a stranger and welcome you, or naked and clothe you? And when did we see you sick or in prison and visit you?' And the King will answer them, 'Truly, I say to you, as you did it to one of the least of these my brothers, you did it to me'" (Matt. 25:37–40).

If we're really interested in answering this question—not just using it as a way to avoid commitment—there is a way to make a start. We can make ourselves available to the poor, the hungry, the homeless, the dying. It means, very concretely, working an evening or morning shift at the shelter for the homeless; it means, concretely, visiting AIDS patients in a hospice; it means doing prison visitation; it means volunteering to help immigrants and refugees.

When we make ourselves available to those who suffer, when we come in humility to help as we can and learn what we must, we will meet Jesus. His form may not be comely—there will be times when his form is that of the crucified. But he will meet us if we're looking for him there.

Mother Teresa said that she saw the face of Jesus in the face of each sick and dying person she helped. One of her prayers put it this way: "Dearest Lord, may I see you today and every day in the person of your sick, and whilst nursing them, minister to you. Though you hide yourself in the unattractive disguise of the irritable, the exacting, and the unreasonable, may I still recognize you and say, 'Jesus, my patient, how sweet it is to serve you.'"[2]

She saw Jesus in the face of the sick and dying not because she was a saint—though she was one—but simply because she looked at so many faces of the sick and dying that eventually she began to recognize her God.

Dietrich Bonhoeffer, the German theologian, reminded us in his *Cost of Discipleship* that those who believe obey, and those who obey believe. This is a profound truth about the spiritual life. Sometimes it is belief that leads into a loving, obedient relationship with Jesus Christ.

But sometimes it works the other way around. We can ponder and pray and wrestle intellectually until we are blue in the soul, and belief will just not come. But if we will obey—if we gamble on Jesus and his Word, if we take the time and effort to visit the sick, go to the prison, spend time with the poor and suffering and look for him there—we will find, surprisingly, mysteriously, wonderfully, that faith grows within us. Like Mother Teresa, we will start recognizing the one who makes himself known in comfort and sorrow, in healing and pain, in resurrection and crucifixion.

And while it will not always make us feel good, even in pain we will know a quiet but steady hope and a subtle but discernable joy. We will be given the knowledge of head and heart that the Grand Canyon of despair has been bridged, that God is not over there and our hurt over here, but they have been brought together in Jesus Christ, and that nothing ever will separate what God has joined together.

15

The Elusive Lover (Mystery)

The LORD has said that he would dwell in thick darkness.

1 Kings 8:12

A book that is supposed to explain God has to, at some point, admit the impossibility of the task. We chafe at this reality. Every spiritual bone in our body rebels against it. Our natural curiosity refuses to submit to it. Our popular theology denies it. This book has, in its own way, been an attempt to explain it away. But the unnerving fact remains: we worship a God shrouded in mystery.

This is something that has taken me a long time to acknowledge, because like many, I have found great delight in learning about and explaining God.

In my college years, I devoured books by apologists like Francis Schaeffer, Paul Little, and C. S. Lewis. This was the seventies, when it was very fashionable at our university, University of California Santa Cruz, to reject "the establishment," which included the Christian religion. I spent many an hour answering the philosophical objections of classmates as we sparred about faith. While this approach failed to convince most of my unbelieving friends, one did become a Christian after college and did so, he said, because as a scientist, he felt the claims of Christian faith made sense.

We are said to live in a postmodern era, in which logical proofs for God's existence and rational explanations of his character are no longer of interest to people. This may be true for some, but classic apologetic books like Josh McDowell's *Evidence That Demands a Verdict* and C. S. Lewis's *Mere Christianity* still sell briskly, and new rationalistic apologists, like Lee Strobel, are widely read and sought as speakers. It seems we have a God-given longing to make sense of God, and all the postmodernism in the world cannot kill it.

But the more I've probed the sensible God, the smaller he seems to get. My head may be able to form answers as to how God is three in one, why Jesus died on the cross, or how a loving and powerful God can allow evil, but the older I've grown, the less my heart is satisfied with these answers. The more I've tried to pinpoint where and how God acts in the world, the less I'm sure of my pinpoints—but nonetheless more sure that God acts.

I also now experience more and more moments when God is profoundly present to me, and yet I increasingly have little idea what exactly is going on when that happens. The more he makes himself known, the more dark he becomes. I feel like Israel at the foot of Mount Sinai:

> On the morning of the third day there were thunders and lightning and a thick cloud on the mountain and a very loud trumpet blast, so that all the people in the camp trembled. Then Moses brought the people out of the camp to meet God, and they took their stand at the foot of the mountain.

Now Mount Sinai was wrapped in smoke because the LORD had descended on it in fire.

Exodus 19:16–18

I hear the thunder and see the lightning of God, but when I try to find God, all I see is smoke. This is what I call a "morning of the third day" event. It was on another morning on the third day that there was an earthquake, the appearance of dazzling angels—and confusion and fear. Mary thought she was talking to a gardener; the disciples did not fathom why the tomb was empty; the disciples on the road to Emmaus were blinded to the one walking with them.

On a recent trip I sat in my eighth-floor hotel room in downtown Ottawa, gazing at an anonymous structure of concrete and steel. What I mostly saw was mirrored glass. It was a tall and imposing structure, impressive in its symmetry, the entire façade made of rectangular windows neatly framed. From where I sat, I could not see the name of the building or tell who owns it or what it might be used for. I could not peer inside to get even a clue, because the windows only reflected back the image of my hotel and the city around and below. One might be tempted to say that this building was nothing more than a reflection of all that goes on around it.

I had reason to believe there was life and energy and power in the building. But I could not penetrate those mirrored windows. The building remained imposing and impressive, and a deep mystery.

Like creation. To be sure, God's "invisible attributes, namely, his eternal power and divine nature, have been clearly perceived, ever since the creation of the world, in the things that have been made. So they are without excuse" (Rom. 1:20). God's presence is sensed, but it's pretty tough to create a profile of a God from a world that includes both daisies and hurricanes, both kittens and rattlesnakes.

The mind can fashion a rational explanation, but the heart remains both perplexed and deeply moved, in fear and trembling and in joyful, inexplicable gratitude.

Why is God so elusive? This is not only personally puzzling but socially embarrassing for those of us who believe in the Judeo-Christian God, the God who is supposed to be in the business of making himself known! We keep telling people that God is near, that God loves them. It would help if he'd show up and at least shake hands when we're trying to introduce him. Instead he often hides behind the door as we yak away about him, motioning him to come on over.

We are sincerely if naively puzzled as to why he doesn't show up on demand. We have Video on Demand. Why can't we have God on Demand? If television producers love us enough to give us what we want when we want it, why can't God, who claims to love us even more than do television producers?

It turns out that God shows his love for us precisely by failing to show up on demand. We will come back to this.

For now we need to recall that the mystery of God is not a new problem. Some tend to think it a product of twentieth-century philosophy and history, the result of our wrestling with mindless evils like the Holocaust and the Gulag: "How can a good God . . . ?" and so forth. People say we now live in a "secular age," and so God is hard to find.[1]

We forget that some of the most evocative expressions of God's elusiveness come from a deeply religious age and people and at the very moments when God is supposedly revealing himself. We just read one description from the book of Exodus. Here is another, from the prophet Ezekiel, who had a vision of God:

> There was the likeness of a throne, in appearance like sapphire; and seated above the likeness of a throne was a likeness

with a human appearance. And upward from what had the appearance of his waist I saw as it were gleaming metal, like the appearance of fire enclosed all around. And downward from what had the appearance of his waist I saw as it were the appearance of fire, and there was brightness around him. Like the appearance of the bow that is in the cloud on the day of rain, so was the appearance of the brightness all around.

Such was the appearance of the likeness of the glory of the LORD.

Ezekiel 1:26–28

Even in this so-called epiphany, God remains shielded by the vague and evasive language Ezekiel is forced to employ: "the likeness of" and "the appearance of." His summary is doubly vague: "Such was the appearance of the likeness . . ." (Ezek. 1:28). In other words, though Ezekiel had a vision of God, God remained hidden.

"To whom then will you liken God, or what likeness compare with him?" says Isaiah as he strains to find ways to describe God (Isa. 40:18). In the end, I think he just gave up: "Truly, you are a God who hides himself" (Isa. 45:15).

Paradoxically, things don't get much better when Jesus—"God with us"—shows up. While he does indeed "show us the Father" in a lot of ways, Jesus, the very revelation of God, talks about God's hiddenness time and again. Note how he talks about the "kingdom of God," that is, the experience of God in all its fullness: It is like a treasure *hidden* in a field (see Matt. 13:44). It is like a field in which both wheat and weeds are so mixed up, you can hardly separate them (see Matt. 13:24–30). It is like a parable, which hides as much as it reveals, which for "outsiders" is given that "they may indeed see but not perceive, and may indeed hear but not understand" (Mark 4:12).

Jesus himself—"God from God, Light from Light, True God from True God," as the Nicene Creed says—remained a stumbling block and an offense from birth to death and resurrection. His own people knew him not. The descriptions of God and heaven in Revelation match the excruciating incoherence of Ezekiel. Paul, after trying to explain God's plan for Israel, throws up his hands and says, "How unsearchable are his judgments and how inscrutable his ways!" (Rom. 11:33).

While God clearly is about the business of giving us glimpses of himself, he is also clearly in the business of hiding himself. This may frustrate us, but I think that it is part of God's wonderful plan for our lives. Only when we accept the ultimate mystery of God can we know and love him.

God hides himself because he does not want to be found if people are apt to mistake him for an idol.

> Truly, you are a God who hides yourself,
>   O God of Israel, the Savior.
> All of them are put to shame and confounded;
>   the makers of idols go in confusion together.
>
> Isaiah 45:15–16

God leaves us confused and confounded whenever we try to make God fit our ideas of who God should be.

Our God is the God who answers prayer—but he is not a divine bellhop who jumps at our every request. He refuses sometimes to hear prayers that are attempts merely to manipulate him.

Our God is full of mercy and love—but he is not the Cosmic Nice Guy. Just when we think we need a pat on the back, he gives us a kick in the rear. Just when we expect a little praise for how much money we raise for him, he gets out a whip and drives us from the temple. Just when we need him most, when we're hanging on a cross, looking for him to strengthen and sustain us like he's supposed to, he is nowhere to be found, even when we cry about feeling utterly forsaken.

To know God, to live with God, to love God, one must be willing to embrace this sort of confusion. It means to be regularly mystified by God. An old bumper sticker described conversion with the phrase I FOUND IT. That is part of the journey of faith. But it should be matched later by another: I LOST IT.

God is beyond everything that exists and every conception we can have of him, says Eastern Orthodox theologian Vladimir Losski. "In order to approach him, it is necessary to deny all that is inferior to him"—especially our small and confined images of who he is. "It is by *unknowing* that one may know him."[2]

I misplaced my keys one day. I looked in each place where they should have been, where I always leave them: in my coat pockets, in my pants pockets, on top of the chest of drawers. I checked and rechecked these places over and over in disbelief that the keys were not to be found in one of those places. Only after many minutes of rising frustration did I give up that search. I then started to look in places where the keys were not likely to be. That's when I found them, lying on a windowsill.

God is often near, right there on the windowsill, but only when we give up our ideas about where he is and how exactly he is to be found will we find him. That's why we can rejoice when we bump into the mystery of God, when God seems more confusing than ever. That's the first, necessary step in discovering where he really is.

The mystery of God also acts like a magnet for us. It is not dissimilar to falling in love.

As I started to fall in love with the woman who was to become my wife, I became increasingly fascinated with her. I wanted to know what books she liked, what hobbies she enjoyed, what her favorite color was. I wondered what her family was like, if she had previous boyfriends, and what goals she had for her life.

The more I probed, the more I became curious: when I learned she had two sisters and a brother, I wanted to know how she got along with each. And once I found that out, I wanted to know why.

A time came in our marriage when, sadly, Barbara no longer seemed a mystery to me. I thought I pretty much had her figured out. I knew her so well, she began to grate on me—her opinions, her habits, her turns of phrase were all so predictable! Instead of longing to be with her more and more, I wanted to get away.

This is a necessary chapter of marriage: we must become disillusioned with the familiar before we can move toward deeper intimacy. The problem was not that Barbara had become boring; it was that I had put her in the Barbara box, a neat little container that defined who she was.

Becoming "born again" is like falling in love, and our spiritual courtship is a series of emotional highs as we discover the manifold wonders of God. But a little knowledge of God is a dangerous thing, and after a while, we think we've got him figured out. And we put God in that neat little container.

Then one day we go to get God out of that container—we expect him to answer a prayer or bless a venture, or we look for an answer to some tragedy we face—and we open it and find he is not there. Just when we needed him, he's up and gone! And we are angry. What happened to my God?

We stomp around the room in a fury, and we pout, and we vow never to be so naive about religion again. And then we start to cry. We remember our first love. Even greater than our desire to manipulate God is our desire to love God. More than wanting to merely use God, we simply want God.

That longing is not only resurrected by the mystery of God, it is heightened by it. We can, yes, say many things that are true about God. We can list and discuss his attributes and learn much in the process. But we will not have grasped God in his attributes until we have recognized that the more we understand them, the more we don't know about God. But the more elusive God is, the more we want him. The more he teases us, the more we chase after him.

This can become the beginning of a new stage of faith, where the mystery of God becomes not a stumbling block and not a puzzle to be solved. It is mystery that ever draws us toward him in both wonder and joy.

A Companion Guide

This companion guide is designed to help groups reflect together on the themes of *A Great and Terrible Love*. It offers a simple guide for groups to follow. It is sparse enough to be easily supplemented with readings, songs, instruction, and other activities, depending on the energy and creativity of those planning the gatherings.

I've included with each chapter's questions a prayer or a collect (a short prayer that sums up the attribute under discussion).

The questions are designed to elicit conversation. They may need to be rearranged or reworded to work best for your own group. I encourage you to begin each discussion with the first two questions below and end with the third. Depending on the group dynamics, that will sometimes be sufficient to generate a meaningful discussion.

- **What sentence, illustration, or idea was most compelling to you?**
- **Where do you find yourself disagreeing with the author in this chapter? Or what is missing from his discussion?**

- **What is one thing you want to take away from this chapter?**

The questions are not designed to lead the group to some designated conclusion—I've already written what I want people to consider. If the chapter under discussion is persuasive, the conversation will end up affirming the theme. If not, I trust some other truth will emerge that will be edifying. When it comes to book discussions, I find I often learn more when I disagree with an author!

Questions mix the theological and the personal. The leader will want to mix and match depending on the personality of the group. In addition, the group can discuss the closing prayer and/or opening quotation in each discussion section.

In any case, an atmosphere of freedom should characterize the discussion. The point of the book—and therefore this companion guide—is to become immersed in the love of our holy God.

Mark Galli

Part 1: Theological Attributes

Chapter 1: Immutable

The first and fundamental difference between the Creator and his creatures is that they are mutable and their nature admits change, whereas God is immutable and can never cease to be what he is.

J. I. Packer[1]

Has God's immutability been a problem for you? If so, has it been more of an intellectual hurdle or a personal one?

What is the problem with conceiving God as one who only responds to human behavior and requests?

What is the problem with conceiving God as one whose plans and purposes have been set "before the foundations of the world"?

While recognizing the paradox of immutability—that God's purposes are unwavering and that he responds to us in prayer—which do you think is most easily neglected in this day and age?

Which part of the paradox do you find yourself more sympathetic to? Which do you want to learn more about?

O God immutable, you continually reach out in unchangeable love toward your feeble and fickle people. Help us to know your steady mercy, that our love for you and others may not diminish nor waver but only become ever more deeply rooted, as we are, in Jesus Christ our Lord. Amen.

Chapter 2: Omnipotent

> Nothing is too hard for Jesus,
> No man can work like him.
>
> an African-
> American spiritual

When have you felt most thankful for God's power or seen his power most manifest?

When have you, like Habakkuk, felt most frustrated by God's seeming lack of power?

Why do you think God has decided to display his power not only in strength but also in weakness?

Which form of God's power—left-handed or right-handed—are you most attracted to? Why?

Where in your life do you now need an "able God"?

O God omnipotent, you are able to do that which you mercifully intend, in apparent weakness and in seeming strength. Help us to know and trust your power, if not fully comprehend it, that we might rest secure in the knowledge that nothing can alter your loving purpose toward us and your creation; through Jesus Christ our Lord. Amen.

Chapter 3: Immanent

The whole universe is a cosmic Burning Bush, filled with the divine Fire yet not consumed.

Bishop Timothy Ware[2]

Describe a time when you have sensed God's immanent presence.

What problems arise if we neglect the transcendence of God in our worship and prayers?

What are the problems of neglecting the immanence of God?

Which part of the transcendent/immanent paradox do you think is most neglected today in the church? In your own life?

Describe a moment or a situation when you have experienced or repeatedly do experience the immanence of God.

Christ with me, Christ before me, Christ behind me, Christ in me!
Christ below me, Christ above me.
Christ at my right, Christ at my left!
Christ in breadth, Christ in length, Christ in height!

from a prayer attributed to Saint Patrick[3]

Chapter 4: Omniscient

Our entire inner life, our thoughts and desires, our feelings and
imaginations, are known to God. . . . The human resistance
against such relentless observation can scarcely be broken.

Paul Tillich[4]

God's omniscience can present problems like those we
encounter with God's immutability. In this case, if God
knows what is going to happen, is there any point in
praying? Has this ever been a question of yours? How
do you resolve this mystery in your own mind?

Some people find God's full knowledge of us comforting;
others find it disturbing. Which is it for you?

Do you agree that when we hide something from ourselves,
we are in essence trying to hide it from God?

Can you talk about a time when you discovered you have
been hiding something of yourself from yourself? In ret-
rospect, do you think this was a way of hiding it from
God?

If we know God is loving and merciful, why do we find it
so hard to admit things to ourselves, even in the privacy
of our own hearts?

What is the most remarkable thing you have discovered
about yourself, only to realize that God knew about this
long before you did and yet still worked in your life?

*O God omniscient, you know our going out and coming in and
the secrets of our hearts before we know them. Help us to rest
in this knowledge as a sign of your everlasting grace, through
the one who lived and died for us before we came into existence,
Jesus Christ our Lord. Amen.*

Chapter 5: Omnipresent

The doctrine of God's omnipresence personalizes man's relation to the universe. . . . God is present, near him, next to him, and knows him through and through. At this point faith begins.

A. W. Tozer[5]

What are the various reasons—human and divine—someone might feel alone and forsaken by God?

Is there a way to discern whether this sense of alienation is primarily due to our sin or is due to the impenetrable will of God?

How is it that we can take something good—the religious practices of a spiritual life—and use them to help us avoid God? Has that ever happened to you?

What do you do daily or weekly to help you become more aware of God's constant presence?

When have you felt forsaken by God? Talk about that time and how you came through it?

O God omnipresent, you are always and everywhere closer to us than we are to ourselves. Help us to discern your merciful presence even when we feel forsaken and alone, so that we might know you as does the one who felt forsaken on the cross, even Jesus Christ our Lord. Amen.

Part 2: Biblical Attributes

Chapter 6: Eternal

> O God, our help in ages past,
> Our hope for years to come,
> Our shelter from the stormy blast,
> And our eternal home.

Isaac Watts[6]

What is it about eternal life that you find the most difficult to fathom or appreciate?

What is the most attractive aspect of eternal life for you?

What everyday activity so absorbs you that you lose track of time, so that you experience some sense of eternity even now?

What to you are the spiritual disciplines and/or activities that most help you experience God's eternal life even now?

What are the things that get in the way of your living with a sense of eternity in your heart day by day?

O God eternal, you have set eternity in our hearts, and our hearts are restless until they rest in you. May we taste the blessings of life everlasting even now, as we make our way on this earth toward the kingdom of heaven, which is already being prepared for us by our eternal Lord and King, Jesus Christ, through whom we pray. Amen.

Chapter 7: Lord

There is one God, one Lord, and his people are defined as those who love him, and who love their neighbors as themselves.

N. T. Wright[7]

What about the attribute "Lord" do you find the hardest to appreciate?

What about it do you find most helpful?

The author outlines a view of the atonement that highlights the role of Christ's lordship. Is this a view of the atonement that resonates with you? Why or why not?

We usually associate the attribute "Lord" with the need for us to be obedient to God. Here the author connects it with intimacy with God. Which makes more sense to you in terms of your own spiritual journey?

What most hinders you from entering into a more intimate relationship with God?

Glory to God in the highest,
and peace to His people on earth.
Lord God, Heavenly King,
Almighty God and Father,
we worship You, we give You thanks,
we praise You for Your glory.
Lord Jesus Christ,
only Son of the Father,
Lord God, Lamb of God,
You take away the sin of the world:
have mercy on us;
You are seated at the right hand of the Father:
receive our prayer.
For You alone are the Holy One,
You alone are the Lord,
You alone are the Most High,
Jesus Christ, with the Holy Spirit,
in the glory of the Father.
Amen.[8]

Chapter 8: Glory

Someone, I was told, at the sight of a very beautiful body [a woman's] felt impelled to glorify the Creator. The sight of it increased his love for God to the point of tears. Anyone who entertains such feelings in such circumstances is already risen . . . before the general resurrection.

John Climacus[9]

What do you think of when you hear the word *glory* or *glorious*? Is this a meaningful word for you?

Does it make sense to you that glory can have overtones of both shining light and something weighty?

Have you had an experience when you sensed God's glory in creation? Explain.

Saint Benedict wrote in his Rule, "Look upon all the tools and all the property of the monastery as if they were sacred altar vessels."[10] What difference would it make in your life if you looked upon your own possessions in this way?

What stands in the way of your having a more vivid sense of God's glory day to day?

> *Glory to you, Lord God of our fathers;*
> *you are worthy of praise; glory to you.*
> *Glory to you for the radiance of your holy Name;*
> *we will praise you and highly exalt you for ever.*
> *Glory to you in the splendor of your temple;*
> *on the throne of your majesty, glory to you.*
> *Glory to you, seated between the Cherubim;*
> *we will praise you and highly exalt you for ever.*
> *Glory to you, beholding the depths;*
> *in the high vault of heaven, glory to you.*
> *Glory to you, Father, Son, and Holy Spirit;*
> *we will praise you and highly exalt you for ever.*[11]

Chapter 9: Righteous

People should not worry as much about what they do but rather about what they are. If they and their ways are good, then their deeds are radiant. If you are righteous, then what you do will also be righteous.

Meister Eckhart[12]

What have been your reactions to the word *righteous* or *righteousness?* Are they mostly negative, like the early Martin Luther's, or positive?

Who is the most righteous person you know? Tell the group about him or her.

How can our desire to act righteously—in the sense of acting morally—get in the way of community and relationships? How can it help those relationships?

The author says, "Thus righteousness is grounded and fulfilled not in morally pure behavior but in relationship. Not primarily in adherence to some abstract set of laws but in the midst of community, the divine community we call the Trinity, the earthly community we call the church. We were created for such community, for relationships, for intimacy, for love. And righteousness is one word that crystallizes all that." What do you think of the argument that led up to this conclusion? In what ways is it a helpful corrective? In what ways might it be misunderstood and confuse people?

O God of righteousness, you have created us to be in a
covenant with you, a Trinity whose love knows no bounds.
Help us to live in the fullness of your righteousness, not only
living upright all our days as you have commanded but
stretching out our arms in love to a hurting world; through
Jesus Christ the Righteous One. Amen.

Chapter 10: Merciful

Heaven have mercy on us all—Presbyterians and Pagans alike—for we are all somehow dreadfully cracked about the head, and sadly need mending.

Herman Melville[13]

The author says, "We can rarely if ever approach God with perfect humility. We're always looking for something from God, always looking to finagle something out of him." Is that true in your experience? If so, is it always bad?

What in your church culture or larger culture implicitly encourages us to think of faith as a quid pro quo ("something for something") with God?

In what aspect of your relationship with God are you tempted to seek a quid pro quo?

What signals to you that you might not be seeking God's mercy but just seeking to feel good or feel spiritual?

How do you react to this sentence in the chapter: "To seek God's mercy means, paradoxically, abandoning any right to mercy and any hope of mercy." Is that freeing or frightening to you?

Lord, be merciful to me, a sinner.
Lord, be merciful to me, a sinner.
Lord, be merciful to me, a sinner.

Lord, have mercy.
Christ, have mercy.
Lord, have mercy. Amen.

Chapter 11: Jealous

You love without burning; you are jealous in a way that is free from anxiety.

Augustine[14]

Tell about a time when you felt the pangs of jealousy. In what ways was it "good jealousy"? In what ways was it not?

169

What signals to you that appropriate jealousy is turning sour?

We associate jealousy with romantic love. In what other contexts can jealousy be either appropriate or destructive?

Other than a romantic relationship or your relationship with God, who or what have you loved most dearly?

If we say we love some person or group but then are never tempted with jealousy, do we *really* love them? Why or why not?

> *Our jealous God, you made us for yourself, and only in you do we know true love and joy. May your zealous love so penetrate our hearts that we no longer will be tempted to forsake you, our first love; through Jesus Christ, Love Incarnate. Amen.*

Chapter 12: Wrath

Mine eyes have seen the glory of the coming of the
    Lord:
He is trampling out the vintage where the grapes of
    wrath are stored.
He hath loosed the fateful lightning of His terrible
    swift sword:
      His truth is marching on.

Julia Ward Howe[15]

Are you instinctively repulsed, fascinated, or comforted by the idea of God's anger? Why?

Describe a time when you or someone else displayed righteous anger.

What things today should Christians have righteous indignation about? Should we have more anger about these things? Why or why not?

Where is Christian righteous indignation displayed inappropriately today?

How can we tell when righteous anger is becoming sinful anger?

How does God's action in Jesus Christ make a difference in how we understand righteous anger?

O God of wrath, your anger burns against all evil and injustice. So fill us with your love so that we too become passionately impatient with anything that prevents us or our neighbors from enjoying your complete goodness; through Jesus Christ our Lord. Amen.

Part 3: Attributes of Love

Chapter 13: Trinity

God is not solitude, but perfect communion. For this reason the human person, the image of God, realizes himself or herself in love, which is a sincere gift of self.

Pope Benedict XVI[16]

Has the doctrine of the Trinity been a meaningful doctrine for you? Why or why not?

Which person of the Trinity do you feel most drawn to? Least drawn to?

The author argues that God doesn't need our love. How do you react to that idea?

Describe a time when your love was an overflow of love rather than mere obedience to a command to love.

Given human nature, we often have to love out of obedience, so that we might grow in love. What should we do, though, if we seem to be stuck in "love as duty" and never give out of the overflow of love?

O God the Three in One, you have existed as a perfect fellowship of love from eternity. Pour yourself into our hearts that love might overflow to others, that we too may know a divine fellowship; in the name of the Father, the Son, and the Holy Spirit. Amen.

Chapter 14: Suffering

The pupil dilates in the dark, and the soul dilates in misfortune and ends by finding God there.

Victor Hugo[17]

What are the types of suffering that you find most inexplicable?

We usually find innocent suffering (like child abuse) the most hard to swallow. Yet Jesus was the only truly innocent person who has suffered. How does that change how we understand innocent suffering?

Most of us avoid suffering—our own and that of others. We do not like to face painful realities about ourselves; we do not like to visit others who are in pain. But we hear time and again that suffering accepted in faith is redemptive and that one does not learn anything in this life except through suffering. Why—aside from the obvious fact that pain hurts—are we tempted to run away from suffering?

How do you normally deal with your own suffering? What mechanisms, healthy and not, do you tend to revert to?

Talk about a time when you met God in the midst of suffering.

Lord Jesus Christ! A whole life long didst thou suffer that I too might be saved; and yet thy suffering is not yet at an end; but this too wilt thou endure, saving and redeeming me, this patient suffering of having to do with me, I who so often go astray from the right path, or even when I remained on the straight path stumbled along it or crept so slowly along the right path. Infinite patience, suffering of infinite patience. How many times have I not been impatient, wished to give up and forsake everything; wished to take the terribly easy way out, despair: but thou didst not lose patience. Oh, I cannot say what thy chosen servant says: that he filled up that which is behind of the afflictions of Christ in his flesh; no, I can only say that I increased thy sufferings, added new ones to those which thou didst once suffer in order to save me.

Søren Kierkegaard[18]

Chapter 15: Mystery

If in seeing God, one can know what one sees, then one has not seen God in himself but something intelligible, something inferior to him. It is by unknowing that one may know him who is above every possible object of knowledge.

Vladimir Lossky[19]

What do you find most incomprehensible about God?

What resources, practices, or insights best help you understand God as much as you can?

Do you think the mystery of God is an attraction or a stumbling block for those outside the church?

Do you think churches today err on the side of making God too familiar or don't do enough to explain the faith clearly?

What do you think are the chief dangers of making God too accessible? Too mysterious?

What can we do to become more comfortable with the mystery of God? Or is mystery by its very nature discomforting?

Come, true light.
Come, life eternal.
Come, hidden mystery.
Come, treasure without name.
Come, person beyond all understanding.
Come, rejoicing without end.
Come, light that knows no evening.
Come, unfailing expectation of the saved.
Come, raising of the fallen.
Come, resurrection of the dead.
Come, all powerful, for unceasingly you create, refashion, and
change all things by your will alone.
Come, invisible whom none may touch or handle.
Come, for you continue always unmoved, yet at every instant
you are wholly in movement; you draw near to us who lie in
hell, yet you remain higher than the heavens.
Come, for your love fills our hearts with longing and is ever on
our lips; yet who you are and what your nature is, we cannot
say or know.
Come, Alone to the alone.
Come, for you are yourself the desire within me.
Come, my breath and my life.
Come, the consolation of my humble soul.
Come, my joy, my glory, my endless delight.

Saint Symeon the Theologian[20]

Notes

Introduction

1. Augustine, *St. Augustine's Confessions*, trans. Henry Chadwick (London: Oxford University Press, 1991), 4.
2. *American Heritage Dictionary of the English Language*, 4th ed., s.v. "terrible," http://www.bartleby.com/61/11/T0121100.html.
3. A. W. Tozer, *The Knowledge of the Holy* (New York: Harper & Row, 1961), 6.
4. Ibid.
5. J. B. Phillips, *Your God Is Too Small* (New York: Macmillan, 1955), vi.
6. Augustine, *Confessions*, 4–5.
7. Ibid.

1. Responsive Control (Immutable)

1. C. H. Spurgeon, "The Immutability of God" (sermon, New Park Street Chapel, Southwark, England, January 7, 1855). Text available online at The Spurgeon Archive, http://www.spurgeon.org/sermons/0001.htm.
2. Richard Rice in Clark Pinnock, Richard Rice, John Sanders, William Hasker, and David Basinger, *The Openness of God* (Downers Grove, IL: InterVarsity, 1994), 25.
3. Søren Kierkegaard, *The Prayers of Kierkegaard*, trans. Perry D. LeFevre (Chicago: University of Chicago Press, 1956), 9.
4. A. W. Tozer, *Knowledge of the Holy* (New York: Harper & Row, 1956), 59.

2. Right- and Left-Handed Power (Omnipotent)

1. *American Heritage Dictionary of the English Language*, 4th ed., s.v. "Power," http://www.bartleby.com/61/20/P0492000.html.
2. Father Leslie Chadd, "God's Left Hand," *New Directions* (February 1997), http://trushare.com/21FEB97/FE97CHAD.htm. This article was originally pub-

lished in 1989 in *Crucible*, the quarterly journal of the Church of England's Board for Social Responsibility.

3. Power Incognito (Immanent)

1. "Praise to the Lord, the Almighty," based on Psalm 103. Written by Joachim Neander in 1680. Translated by Catherine Winkworth in 1863. The words can be found on many websites, including The Cyber Hymnal, http://www.cyberhymnal.org/htm/p/t/pttlta.htm.

Other verses from the hymn are well worth reading in the context of this chapter:

Praise to the Lord, the Almighty, the King of creation!
O my soul, praise Him, for He is thy health and salvation!
All ye who hear, now to His temple draw near;
Praise Him in glad adoration.

Praise to the Lord, who over all things so wondrously reigneth,
Shelters thee under His wings, yea, so gently sustaineth!
Hast thou not seen how thy desires ever have been
Granted in what He ordaineth?

Praise to the Lord, who hath fearfully, wondrously, made thee;
Health hath vouchsafed and, when heedlessly falling, hath stayed thee.
What need or grief ever hath failed of relief?
Wings of His mercy did shade thee.

Praise to the Lord, who doth prosper thy work and defend thee;
Surely His goodness and mercy here daily attend thee.
Ponder anew what the Almighty can do,
If with His love He befriend thee.

2. John of Damascus, as quoted in Vladimir Lossky, *The Mystical Theology of the Eastern Church* (Crestwood, NY: St. Vladimir's Seminary Press, 1976), 36.

3. Ibid., 25.

4. Versions of this prayer can be found readily all over the Web. This one is taken from the Order of Saint Patrick website, http://orderofsaintpatrick.org/breastplate.htm.

5. This version of the "Canticle" has been taken from *Francis and Clare: The Complete Works*, in the Classics of Western Spirituality series, translation and introduction by Regis J. Armstrong, OFM, Cap. and Ignatius C. Brady, OFM (New York: Paulist Press, 1986), 37.

6. Julian of Norwich, *Revelations of Divine Love*, trans. Clifton Wolters (London: Penguin Books, 1966), 68.

7. As quoted in Bishop Kallistos Ware, *The Orthodox Way* (Crestwood, NY: St. Vladimir's Seminary Press, 1979, 1993), 58. For much of the discussion in this chapter, I am indebted to Bishop Ware's discussion in this book, especially pages 54–60.

8. Ibid., 157.

4. All-Knowing Grace (Omniscient)

1. Paul Tillich, "Escape from God," in *The Shaking of the Foundations* (New York: Charles Scribner's Sons, 1955). This sermon is now in the public domain. A version can be found on the GodWeb website at http://www.godweb.org/shaking.htm.

5. The Presence of the Forsaken (Omnipresent)

1. David Van Biema, "Mother Teresa's Crisis of Faith," *Time*, August 23, 2007, http://www.time.com/time/world/article/0,8599,1655415,00.html.

6. The Everlasting Now (Eternal)

1. Grace Jantzen, "Time and Timelessness," in *New Dictionary of Christian Theology*, ed. Alan Richardson and John Bowden (London: SCM Press, 1983), as quoted in William Lane Craig, "Divine Timelessness and Personhood," an essay that can be found at the Leadership U website at http://www.leaderu.com/offices/billcraig/docs/timelessness-personhood.html.

2. David Miller, "Empiricism and Process Theology: God Is What God Does," *The Christian Century*, March 24, 1976, 284–87. An online version can be found at Religion-Online, http://www.religion-online.org/showarticle.asp?title=1837.

3. George Eldon Ladd, *A Theology of the New Testament* (Grand Rapids: Eerdmans, 1974), 290.

4. William Shakespeare, *Antony and Cleopatra*, act 1, scene 3, lines 36–37. This scene can be read online on many sites, including About.com, http://shakespeare.about.com/library/blantony_1_3.htm.

5. Saint John of the Cross, *Dark Night of the Soul*, trans. E. Allison Peers (Mineola, NY: Dover Publications, 2003), 2. More such experiences are analyzed by Evelyn Underhill in her classic *Mysticism: The Preeminent Study in the Nature and Development of Spiritual Consciousness* (New York: Doubleday, 1990).

7. Liberating Love (Lord)

1. Arnaldo Fortini, *Francis of Assisi*, trans. Helen Moak (New York: Crossroad, 1992), 154.

2. A longer description of this incident can be found in Mark Galli, *Francis of Assisi and His World* (Oxford: Lion Publishing, 2002), 13–27.

3. Ronald Rolheiser, *The Holy Longing: The Search for a Christian Spirituality* (New York: Doubleday, 1999), 3.

4. Augustine, *Confessions*, 3.

5. Rosemary Radford Ruether, "Christology and Feminism: Can a Male Saviour Save Women?" in *To Change the World* (New York: Crossroad, 1981), 48–49. It can be accessed on the website Women Priests: The Case for Ordaining Women in the Catholic Church, www.womenpriests.org/theology/reuther1.asp.

6. Ibid., 48.

7. Ibid.

8. Gustav Aulen, *Christus Victor: An Historical Study of the Three Main Types of the Idea of Atonement*, trans. A. G. Herber (New York: Macmillan, 1977), 20.

8. The Weight of Light (Glory)

1. For the following discussion, I am endebted to Olivier L. Clément, "The Glory of God Hidden in His Creatures," from *The Roots of Christian Mysticism*, trans. Theodore Berkeley (New York: New City, 1993). It can be accessed on the MyrioBiblio Library website: http://www.myriobiblos.gr/texts/english/clement_1.html.

2. A Monk of the Eastern Church, *Love without Limits* (Belgium: Chevetogne, 1971), 27–28.

3. Maximus the Confessor, *Ambigua* (PG 91: 1288).

4. Benedict of Nursia, *Rule*, XXI, 10 (Centenario, p. 76).

5. Isaac of Nineveh, *Ascetic Treatises*, 72 (p. 281).

6. Evagrius of Pontus, *Practicus* or *The Monk* (SC 171, p. 694).

7. Gregory the Great, *Dialogues*, 35 (PL 66: 198–200).

9. The Kiss of Community (Righteous)

1. From a table talk in 1538, as found in *The Career of the Reformer IV*, vol. 34 of *Luther's Works*, ed. Lewis W. Spitz, trans. Helmut T. Lehmann (Philadelphia: Fortress Press, 1960), 308–9.

2. Ibid., 336–37.

3. For the following discussion, I am indebted to an article on "righteousness" in *New Dictionary of Theology*, ed. David F. Wright, Sinclair B. Ferguson, and J. I. Packer (Downers Grove, IL: InterVarsity Press, 1988), 590–92; and to an article by N. T. Wright, "Justification: The Biblical Basis and Its Relevance for Contemporary Evangelicalism," in *The Great Acquittal: Justification by Faith and Current Christian Thought*, ed. Gavin Reid (London: Collins, 1980), 13, as found on the website NTWrightPage.com, www.ntwrightpage.com/Wright_Justification_Biblical_Basis.pdf.

10. Beyond Manipulation (Merciful)

1. "Mr. John Bunyan's Dying Sayings," from the 1861 edition of *Bunyan's Works*, as found on the Acacia John Bunyan Library website, http://acacia.pair.com/Acacia.John.Bunyan/Sermons.Allegories/Bunyan.Dying.Sayings/1.html.

11. Fierce Passion (Jealous)

1. Marilynne Robinson, *Gilead* (New York: Farrar, Straus & Giroux, 2004), 125.

2. Earlier Rule, 8.3, as found in *The Saint*, vol. 1 of *Francis of Assisi: Early Documents*, ed. Regis J. Armstrong, J. A. Wayne Hellmann, and William Short (New York: New City, 2000), 69.

3. Ibid., 8.7, 70.

4. A Mirror of Perfection, 14, as found in *The Prophet*, vol. 3 of *Francis of Assisi: Early Documents*, ed. Regis J. Armstrong, J. A. Wayne Hellmann, and William Short (New York: New City, 1999), 266.

5. Earlier Rule, 13.6, 83.

12. Redeeming Anger (Wrath)

1. Julia Ward Howe, "The Battle Hymn of the Republic."
2. Abraham Lincoln, second inaugural address.
3. Dorothy Sayers, "The Greatest Drama Ever Staged," Project Gutenberg Canada, March 2008, http://www.gutenberg.ca/ebooks/sayers-greatest/sayers-greatest-00-h.html. Originally published in London by Hodder and Stoughton in 1938.

13. Life That Bubbles Over (Trinity)

1. The Athanasian Creed, text of the International Consultation on English Texts (ICET) and the English Language Liturgical Consultation (ELLC). This creed can be found on many websites, including that of the Evangelical Lutheran Church in America: www.elca.org/what-we-believe/statements-of-belief/the-Athanasian-Creed.aspx.
2. This symbol and its explanation can be found in many books and websites. One particularly good website is the Wikipedia entry: http://en.wikipedia.org/wiki/Shield_of_the Trinity.
3. The following is adapted from Mark Galli, *Beyond Bells & Smells: The Wonder and Power of Christian Liturgy* (Brewster, MA: Paraclete Press, 2008), 87–89.
4. For the following I'm indebted to Bishop Timothy Ware for a section titled "Partakers of the Divine Nature" in *The Orthodox Church* (New York: Penguin, 1993), 231–38.
5. Ibid., 237.

14. Bridge Over the Chasm of Despair (Suffering)

1. Lyn S. Graybill, *Truth and Reconciliation in South Africa: Miracle or Model?* (Boulder, CO: Lynne Reinner Publishers, 2002), 43, 45, and 44, respectively.
2. Mother Teresa, quoted in *The Oxford Book of Prayer*, ed. George Appleton (Oxford: Oxford University Press, 1985), 133.

15. The Elusive Lover (Mystery)

1. See especially Charles Taylor's *A Secular Age* (Cambridge, MA: Belknap Press, 2007), in which he shows how the modern era is unique in that the question of God's existence is genuinely up for grabs in a way it never has been before.
2. Vladimir Lossky, *The Mystical Theology of the Eastern Church* (Crestwood, NY: St. Vladimir's Seminary Press, 1957), 25.

A Companion Guide

1. J. I. Packer, *Knowing God* (Downers Grove, IL: InterVarsity Press, 1973), 69.
2. Ware, *The Orthodox Way*, 157.
3. Versions of this prayer can be found readily all over the Web. This one is taken from the Order of Saint Patrick website, http://orderofsaintpatrick.org/breastplate.htm.

4. Paul Tillich, "Escape from God," in *The Shaking of the Foundations* sermon, now in the public domain. A version can be found on the GodWeb website at http://www.godweb.org/shaking.htm.

5. A. W. Tozer, *Knowledge of the Holy*, 81.

6. Isaac Watts, "Our God, Our Help in Ages Past," 1719, as found on the Cyber Hymnal website, http://www.cyberhymnal.org/htm/o/g/ogohiap.htm.

7. N. T. Wright, "One God, One Lord, One People: Incarnational Christology for a Church in a Pagan Environment," *Ex Audito* 7 (1991), http://www.npcts.edu/sem/exauditu/papers/wright.html.

8. This prayer is called "Glory to God" and can be found in many versions in worship books across many denominations. This one is from Catholic Online, http://www.catholic.org/prayers/prayer.php?p=785.

9. John Climacus, The Ladder of Divine Ascent, 15th step, 58.

10. Benedict of Nursia, *Rule*, XXI, 10 (Centenario, p. 76).

11. "A Song of Praise" or B*enedictus es, Domine*, from *The Book of Common Prayer* (New York: The Church Hymnal Corporation, 1979), 96.

12. *Meister Eckhart: Selected Writings*, trans. Oliver Davies (New York: Penguin Books, 1995), 7.

13. Herman Melville, *Moby Dick*. This classic American novel is now in the public domain and can be accessed on many sites on the Internet, like Infomotions: http://infomotions.com/alex2/authors/melville-herman/melville-moby-743/. This version originally published in 2005 by Infomotions, Inc. This document is distributed under the GNU Public License.

14. Augustine, *Confessions*, 5.

15. Julia Ward Howe, "Battle Hymn of the Republic," 1862. The words to this classic American hymn can be found on many websites, including The Atlantic Online, http://www.theatlantic.com/issues/1862feb/batthym.htm.

16. Pope Benedict XVI, "Angelus," homily delivered on Solemnity of the Most Holy Trinity, May 22, 2005, as found on the Vatican website, http://www.vatican.va/holy_father/benedict_xvi/angelus/2005/documents/hf_ben-xvi_ang_20050522_holy-trinity_en.html.

17. Victor Hugo, *Les Miserables*, trans. Isabel F. Hapgood, Volume V, Book III, Chapter I. Available online at Project Gutenberg, text created by Judith Boss, May 1994, last updated April 17, 2005, http://www.gutenberg.org/dirs/etext94/lesms10.txt.

18. Kierkegaard, *The Prayers of Kierkegaard*, 80.

19. Lossky, *Mystical Theology of the Eastern Church*, 25.

20. Saint Symeon the Theologian, quoted in *The Oxford Book of Prayer*, ed. George Appleton (Oxford: Oxford University Press, 1985), 181–82.

Mark Galli is senior managing editor of *Christianity Today.* His recent books include *Jesus Mean and Wild: The Unexpected Love of an Untamable God* (Baker) and *Beyond Smells and Bells: The Wonder and Power of Christian Liturgy* (Paraclete). Formerly a Presbyterian pastor, he is now a member of an Anglican parish, Church of the Resurrection in Wheaton, Illinois.

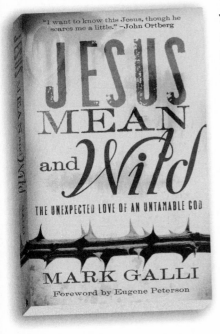
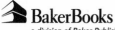